A SENECA INDIAN IN THE UNION ARMY

The Civil War Letters of Sergeant Isaac Newton Parker,

1861 - 1865

Edited by
Laurence M. Hauptman

Burd Street Press a division of
White Mane Publishing Co., Inc.

This Burd Street Press book
was printed by
Beidel Printing House, Inc.
63 West Burd Street
Shippensburg, PA 17257 USA

In respect for the scholarship contained herein, the acid-free paper used in this book meets the guidelines for permanence and durability of the Committee on Production Guidelines for Book Longevity of the Council on Library Resources.

For a complete list of available publications
please write
Burd Street Press
Division of White Mane Publishing Company, Inc.
P.O. Box 152
Shippensburg, PA 17257 USA

Library of Congress Cataloging-in-Publication Data

Parker, Isaac Newton, b. 1833.
    A Seneca Indian in the Union Army : the Civil War letters of
Sergeant Isaac Newton Parker, 1861-1865 / edited by Laurence M.
Hauptman.
        p.   cm. -- (Civil War heritage series ; v. 5)
    Includes index.
    ISBN 0-942597-57-5 (alk. paper)
    1. Parker, Isaac Newton, b. 1833--Correspondence.   2. United
States--History--Civil War, 1861-1865--Participation, Indian.
3. United States. Army. New York Infantry Regiment, 132nd
(1862-1865). Company D.   4. United States--History--Civil War,
1861-1865--Personal narratives.   5. New York (State)--History--Civil
War, 1861-1865--Personal narratives.   6. Seneca Indians-
-Correspondence.   I. Hauptman, Laurence M.   II. Title.
III. Series.
E540.I3P37   1995
973.7'447--dc20   95-9179
                                                               CIP

For Ramona W. Charles and
Jeanne Marie Jemison,
two who have fought many battles
far from Dixie
for the benefit of their Seneca peoples.

TABLE OF CONTENTS

ILLUSTRATIVE MATERIALS

CHART

MAPS

PHOTOGRAPHS

7

ACKNOWLEDGMENTS

The editor wishes to express his gratitude to a number of people who made this project possible. Mr. George Hamell, a scholar at the New York State Museum, was especially helpful in locating Parker print and photographic materials in private and public collections. He was most gracious in sharing with me his special knowledge of the Parker family. Mr. William Evans of the New York State Archives and Mr. James Corsaro of the Manuscript Division of the New York State Library helped introduce me to their vast holdings on Native Americans and military history. Ms. Mary Bell and Ms. Pat Virgil of the Buffalo and Erie County Historical Society did everything possible to bring this project to fruition. They introduced me to the largest body of Isaac Newton Parker documents, answered my inquiries about them, and allowed them to be included in this collection. Many other librarians and archivists too numerous to mention by name, from New York City to San Marino, California, and from Ottawa, Ontario to Washington, D.C. contributed to this project.

Fellow scholars as well as numerous friends contributed significantly to the project. Reverend William H. Armstrong of Burton, Ohio graciously shared with me his special knowledge of the Parker family and their acquaintances. Dr. Elisabeth Tooker, Emeritus Professor of Anthropology at Temple University, provided detailed critiques of this manuscript at two early stages of its development. My friend David Jaman of Gardiner, New York patiently allowed me to talk incessantly about Newt Parker and his participation in the Civil War. Friends at the Allegany, Cattaraugus, and Tonawanda Indian reservations also contributed to this project. I want to especially thank Ms. Jeanne Marie Jemison and Ms. Ramona W. Charles for their constant encouragement of my research in Native American history. Ms. Abigail Laura Wheeler, the closest living relative of Nicholson Parker, helped enlighten me about her remarkable family. Mr. Duwayne

Duce Bowen and Ms. Judith Greene of the Seneca-Iroquois National Museum also aided me in my research about Native American involvement in the Civil War.

The State University of New York College at New Paltz helped facilitate the completion of this project. During the Spring of 1993, I was awarded a sabbatical leave to work on Iroquois history in the era of the Civil War. Librarians at the College's Sojourner Truth Library answered my persistent questions and provided me with interlibrary loan services which facilitated the completion of this book. Moreover, over the past five years, Joan Walker, the secretary of the History Department, has typed numerous letters of inquiry searching for correspondence written by or about Isaac Newton Parker.

Most importantly, I should like to thank my wife, Ruth, and my two teenage children, Beth and Eric, for bearing with me during the painful process of traveling to do research and editing this manuscript.

Laurence M. Hauptman
New Paltz, New York
May 18, 1994

EDITORIAL PROCEDURES: SCOPE AND METHOD

The Letters

This collection of Isaac Newton Parker's Civil War correspondence contains twenty-nine of his letters, fragments of letters, and notations. Three other letters, not written by Parker but included in this volume, add to our understanding of the Seneca sergeant's military experiences. The originals of these thirty-two documents are housed in four major repositories—the American Philosophical Society, the Buffalo and Erie County Historical Society, the National Archives, and the New York State Library. They were uncovered while undertaking research for my book, *The Iroquois in the Civil War: From Battlefield to Reservation*.[1]

Parker sent thirty-one letters, twenty-four of which have been transcribed here, to his wife Sara Adelaide Jemison, from the time of his initial enlistment in 1861 to early in 1864. Two others were sent to his sister-in-law Martha Hoyt Parker, one to his sister Caroline Parker, and one to missionary Asher Wright; one other was Parker's notations on a map of the Battle of Batchelder's [Batchelor's] Creek in early February, 1864. Twenty-five of the letters were signed and one initialed by the Seneca sergeant. Unfortunately, because of the illegibility of some of his letters to his wife—Parker used pencil in his earliest letters—the editor was unable to transcribe seven of his letters.

The largest body of Isaac Newton Parker manuscripts are deposited at the Buffalo and Erie County Historical Society. In this collection, there are fifty-four letters and fragments of letters in three folders of correspondence, a physical description of Parker, as well as his volunteer enlistment

11

papers. These documents, including twenty-four reproduced in the present volume, are part of the Roy Nagle-Goldome Bank Collection which was purchased by the Society in 1976 with funds contributed by the Buffalo Savings Bank. Nagle, a local historian and well-known raconteur on Buffalo history, had worked for the *Buffalo Courier–Express*, became a realtor, and later served as the sales manager for radio station WBEN. Until his death in 1974, he collected over twenty-five thousand articles, books, documents, pamphlets, photographs, and slides. He was also adopted into the Wolf Clan by Seneca Indians in 1970 and was a winner of the Red Jacket Medal.[2]

The American Philosophical Society has eight Isaac Newton Parker letters and his notations on a map of the Battle of Batchelder's Creek in February, 1864. These documents are part of the six hundred items in the Ely S. Parker Collection acquired in several accessions from Arthur C. Parker, the noted anthropologist, in 1950. Arthur C. Parker, of Seneca descent, was both Ely's and Isaac Newton's great-nephew as well as Ely's biographer.[3] All of Isaac Newton Parker's legible letters and notations that bear on his Civil War military service from both the Buffalo and Erie County Historical Society and the American Philosophical Society are reproduced in the present volume.

While researching the Civil War pension records of Iroquois soldiers housed in the National Archives in Washington, D.C., the editor uncovered another letter written by Parker. In the pension file of Foster J. Hudson, a Seneca sergeant killed in the Civil War, the editor found a letter which Parker wrote to Asher Wright, the famous Presbyterian missionary to the Seneca, notifying him of Hudson's death. That important letter is also reproduced in this collection.[4]

In searching through Parker's compiled military service record in the National Archives, the editor secured a copy of an original autographed letter written by Lewis Henry Morgan, the "father of American anthropology" and friend of the Parker family, recommending the Seneca sergeant for promotion.[5] A second letter, one written to Parker by Chauncey C. Jemison, a Seneca farmer, teacher, and longtime friend of the Parker family, was located in a private collection held by an antique dealer in western New York. This letter has recently been purchased by the New York State Library and has been accessioned by its manuscript division. This significant letter, which is also reproduced in this collection, reveals the prejudice of the era that existed in the recruitment of Iroquois soldiers; it also shows the legal and extralegal efforts by some Iroquois and non-Indians alike to recruit Indian troops for the war effort.[6]

This collection does not claim to be all-inclusive in reproducing every existing letter written by Isaac Newton Parker; however, every attempt was made to track down all of his Civil War correspondence. Over the past eight years, the editor combed every major repository on the Iroquois from Ottawa, Ontario to Washington, D.C., and from Albany, New York to San Marino, California in order to locate Parker letters. Inquiries about Parker were made at tribal museums at Salamanca, New York; Tahlequah, Oklahoma; and Brantford, Ontario. He has employed his contacts with military historians to uncover the elusive life of Isaac Newton Parker. This process was aided by the editor's membership in the Capital District Civil War Roundtable based in Albany, New York, which has allowed him to make valuable contacts with other Civil War roundtables in Baltimore and Buffalo and provided him with the names of the major collectors and private dealers of Civil War memorabilia. Since the aim from the inception of the project was to locate and publish all available Parker letters written during the Civil War, the editor has carefully combed regimental morning reports, muster rolls, order books, town rosters of Civil War recruits, as well as Grand Army of the Republic correspondence for Parker letters and/or for clues about this mysterious man.

TREATMENT OF THE TEXT

This collection follows guidelines for editing diplomatic transcriptions set forth in Mary-Jo Kline's *A Guide to Documentary Editing*, prepared for the Association for Documentary Editing.[7] But the editor has adopted a less intrusive policy of editing the letters wherever possible, avoiding lengthy analysis of each letter and limiting the number of end-of-item footnotes. Although some letters contain significant information in only a few sentences or a paragraph, the editor chose to publish the entire letter. Major persons mentioned in the letters have been identified but without adding excessive informational annotation since a lengthy introduction on Parker's Civil War years is provided. A few clearly defined standards in emending the source's transcriptions were followed. Letters were placed in chronological order, thus interspersing several distinct collections of correspondence. Datelines for letters were put at the beginning of the text, no matter where the date appeared in the source. Each of the letter's salutation, complimentary close, spacing between lines, and indentation in Parker's handwritten source texts were standardized in order to achieve consistency of visual pattern. Moreover, the editor has made uniform all dashes of varying dimensions used in the letters and he has provided a separate chart to indicate the meaning of Parker's abbreviations and shorthand, most of which were Indian or military in origin. No attempt to correct Parker's grammar, misspellings, or erratic punctuation has been made except where necessary for the clarity of meaning of the letter since corrections might hide the uniqueness of Parker's words.

Scholars in need of more precision should consult the original letters at the American Philosophical Society, Buffalo and Erie County Historical Society, the National Archives, and the New York State Library. Indeed, the editor finds the advice of Lyman H. Butterfield quite sound:

> Except for critical texts and documents of special philological interest, such literalness would seem to be neither necessary nor wholly desirable. It does not, of course, present the documents 'as they were written' for type cannot simulate handwriting, and all printed texts must compromise in greater or less degree with their autograph originals.[8]

EDITORIAL SYMBOLS
EMPLOYED IN THE TEXT

[ ]	blanks in the text
[– –]	undecipherable words in text; each dash representing one word
~~canceled text~~	material crossed out by INP

EDITOR'S ABBREVIATIONS EMPLOYED
IN THE TEXT AND THE NOTES

ALI	=	Autograph letter initialed
ALS	=	Autograph letter signed
APS	=	American Philosophical Society, Philadelphia
BECHS	=	Buffalo and Erie County Historical Society, Buffalo
CWPR	=	Civil War Pension Records, National Archives, Washington, D.C.
ESP	=	Ely S. Parker
GAR	=	Grand Army of the Republic
INP	=	Isaac Newton Parker [Roy Nagle—Goldome Bank Collection]
MR	=	Microfilm reel
NA	=	National Archives, Washington, D.C.
NYSL	=	New York State Library, Manuscript Division, Albany
OIA, M234	=	Office of Indian Affairs (Central Office), Correspondence and Related Records. Letters Received, 1824-1880, Microfilm Publication 234
OR	=	United States War Department (comp.), *War of the Rebellion: A Compilation of the Official Records of the Union and Confederate Armies*. 128 vols. Washington, D.C., U.S.G.P.O., 1880-1901.
RG	=	Record Group

ISAAC NEWTON PARKER'S ABBREVIATIONS AND SHORTHAND USED IN HIS LETTERS:

agt.	=	agent
ann.	=	annuity
Brig.	=	Brigadier
Capt.	=	Captain
Catt.	=	Cattaraugus Indian Reservation
Co.	=	Company
Col.	=	Colonel
Dep't	=	Department
Gen'l	=	General
H.'Qrs	=	Headquarters
N.Y.V.	=	New York Volunteers
Rebs	=	rebels
Res	=	reservation
Sergt	=	Sergeant

INTRODUCTION

From the earliest days of European settlement, American Indians were usually pictured as the instigators of conflict. By the nineteenth century, they were often deemed as hostiles and/or renegades intent on "savage war." In reality, as Richard Slotkin has brilliantly written, the "accusation is better understood as an act of psychological projection that made the Indians scapegoats for the morally troubling side of American expansion." It became "a basic ideological convention of a culture that was itself increasingly devoted to the extermination or appropriation of the Indians...."[1] Viewing Indians as hostile enemies ignores a major reality, namely that from the earliest colonial era onward, Native Americans were also allies of the Euro-American world.

At least twenty thousand American Indians were in military service during the Civil War. Yet, Native Americans are an important but neglected area of Civil War historiography. From Annie Heloise Abel's three-volume classic written between 1915 and 1925 to more modern treatments such as Alvin M. Josephy, Jr.'s *The Civil War in the West* (1991), historians have almost exclusively focused on the Five Civilized Tribes—the Cherokee, Chickasaw, Choctaw, Creek, and Seminole—and their military role in Indian Territory and environs; however, the war was a much larger reality for American Indians, affecting communities east as well as west of the Mississippi River.

Bell I. Wiley, the noted military historian, in his two-volume classic on the "common soldier" of the Civil War, quickly dismissed the role of Native Americans. Although acknowledging their helpful service as scouts and in raiding, he concluded that their contributions to the Confederate States of America "was admittedly insignificant and marked by large-scale defection." While recognizing Indian gallantry in combat for the Union, Wiley insisted that the Indians "were often slovenly in dress, careless of equipment, neglectful of camp duties and indifferent to prescribed routine...." Wiley added: "They also seemed inclined at times to support the side which appeared in strongest force among them."[2]

19

American Indians played a more significant role in the Civil War than Wiley's conclusions suggest. While some American Indians tried to survive by avoiding participation in the war, many others contributed to Union and Confederate causes on both land and sea, as laborers in shipyards, as "grunts" in the trenches, and even as commissioned and noncommissioned officers. Two of their number—Ely S. Parker, a Seneca sachem and Union general, and Stand Watie, a Cherokee chief and Confederate general—were among the most distinguished commissioned officers of the war. Indeed, American Indians had diverse reasons for volunteering and quite varied experiences during the war itself, and there were many other communities, including those far from Indian Territory, involved directly in the war effort. For example, forty-nine Oneida from the Green Bay area served in the 14th Wisconsin Volunteer Infantry and were involved in the Atlanta campaign. The 1st Michigan Sharpshooters, composed of a large contingent of Ottawa troops, fought in some of the bloodiest fighting of the war, providing heroic service from the Battle of Spotsylvania to the Battle of the Crater in 1864. Ojibwa Indians, serving in the 9th Minnesota Volunteer Infantry, played a key role covering the Union retreat at Brice's Crossroads. Penobscot Indians from Maine, totaling one-fifth of their community's population, volunteered for service in the Union army and navy. On the opposing side, Catawbas volunteered for service in the 12th South Carolina Infantry, while Lumbee were forced against their will to provide labor for

ELY S. PARKER, 1863
Buffalo and Erie County Historical Society

construction of Confederate fortifications along the South Atlantic coast. Moreover, William Holland Thomas raised four companies of North Carolina Cherokee, the so-called "Thomas Legion," which operated as units in the Confederate army in the mountainous country of western North Carolina and eastern Tennessee.[3]

The Civil War letters of Isaac Newton Parker, a Seneca Indian, provide an important glimpse of Native American life in the Union army. In sharp contrast to the correspondence of his famous brother Ely S. Parker who served as General Grant's military secretary, Isaac Newton Parker's letters reveal more of the experiences of the average Indian

WILLIAM PARKER
Father of Ely S. Parker
From a daguerreotype
Buffalo and Erie County Historical Society

ELIZABETH PARKER
Mother of Ely S. Parker
From a daguerreotype
Buffalo and Erie County Historical Society

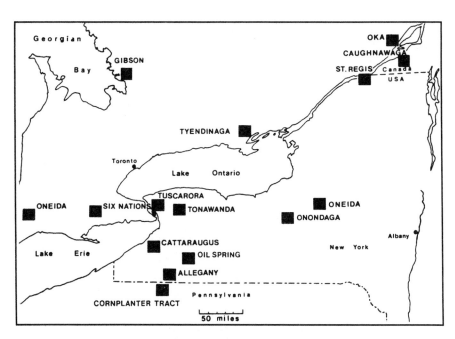

EASTERN IROQUOIS RESERVATIONS, 1860
Jo Margaret Mano, cartographer

foot soldier during this great conflict. "Newt," as he called himself, was the 3rd Sergeant and Color Bearer of D Company of the 132nd New York State Volunteer Infantry and was stationed in the vicinity of New Bern, North Carolina from 1863 to 1865, guarding the rails at this major transportation nexus. Unlike Ely who served as the sole Indian at the power center of the Union high command in 1864 and 1865, Newt served with 24 other Iroquois and in an integrated unit which was popularly called "the Tuscarora Company."[4]

Only one previous historian—W. David Baird—has attempted to provide an edited first-person account of an American Indian during this conflict; however, Baird's work is entirely based on a Creek chief in the Indian Territory as well as Native American involvement in the Confederate army. Moreover, unlike the present study, Baird's important account focuses on life well beyond the Civil War and on the top military echelons, not on the more mundane life of a soldier and his day-to-day camp experiences.[5]

Unlike Baird's study, the present work is a first-person account by an educated Native American in the Union army who was stationed in the East. Parker's letters are also important because they describe every aspect of an Indian soldier's involvement in the conflict: recruitment, training, company life, and combat. They also deal with the harsh realities of war including racial prejudice in recruitment, loneliness, and deaths of trusted comrades. Parker was one of a handful of Seneca in this period of time thoroughly versed in both the Indian and non-Indian worlds. Since he was the best educated Indian in the company, Parker's responsibility was not just to keep his wife Sara Adelaide Jemison or other family members informed, but was also to report on the momentous events occurring in Dixie and on the well-being of the other Iroquois men at war.

Born in 1833, Isaac Newton Parker was the son of Chief William Parker, *Jo-no-es-sto-wa*, a Seneca who had been wounded in battle in the War of 1812. His mother, Elizabeth Johnson, *Ga-out-gwut-twus*, was the niece of Jimmy Johnson, a disciple of the Seneca prophet Handsome Lake. Newt was the second youngest child of six brothers and a sister. He was a product of the Seneca world of Tonawanda, the Baptist mission school there, and the New York State Normal School at Albany. Previous to his enlistment in the war effort, he had been a farmer and a teacher, and had traveled extensively throughout the eastern half of the United States as an entertainer in a troupe with his brother Nicholson.[6]

Little is known about Isaac Newton Parker's appearance. Two daguerreotypes, which are reproduced in this collection, purport to be images of Parker taken in the early 1850s. Housed in the collections of the

New York Public Library and the Missouri Historical Society, they have been recently identified as Parker by scholars Elisabeth Tooker of Temple University, William C. Sturtevant of the Smithsonian Institution, and George Hamell of the New York State Museum, after having been mislabeled and misidentified by other scholars for many years. Union army records indicate that Isaac Newton Parker was 5'8¼" tall, approximately the average height for a soldier during the Civil War, and that he had black hair, dark eyes, and dark complexion.[7]

In the period of Parker's youth, the Seneca Indians faced one of the worst crises in their history, affecting their lands and tribal existence. In 1826, 75 percent of the Tonawanda Reservation, which had been established in 1797 by the Treaty of Big Tree, was sold off by the Seneca. In January, 1838, at

NICHOLSON HENRY PARKER
Son of William and brother of Ely
Photo taken 1892
Buffalo and Erie County Historical Society

the blatantly corrupt Treaty of Buffalo Creek, initiated by the Ogden Land Company and its supporters, and consummated through alcohol, bribery, forgery, and intimidation, the Tonawanda Seneca were defrauded of their remaining lands. Despite appeals to overturn the 1838 treaty, a second treaty in 1842, the so-called "Compromise Treaty," formally recognized the legality of the sale of the Tonawanda as well as the Buffalo Creek Reservations. For the next decade and a half, the Tonawanda Seneca attempted through legal action to overturn the Treaty of 1842. Through the efforts of their attorney John

ISAAC NEWTON PARKER
New York Public Library

Martindale, a white man who later served as the commanding general of the military district of Washington, D.C. during the Civil War, the Tonawanda Seneca's case reached the United States Supreme Court. Before its adjudication, the United States Senate had worked out a resolution of the continuing controversy by allowing the Tonawanda Seneca to use money set aside for the Indians' removal to Kansas. With this money, the Indians purchased back 7,500 acres of tribal lands from the Ogden Land Company. This "settlement" was confirmed in a new federal treaty with the Tonawanda Seneca in 1857.[8]

ISAAC NEWTON PARKER
Missouri Historical Society

Isaac Newton Parker and his family were witnesses to these events and lobbied to regain tribal lands. During this time, they also came in contact with many prominent people of the day who visited the family's homestead. One of the frequent guests was Lewis Henry Morgan who was aided by the Parkers, including Newt, in producing his ground-breaking ethnography, *The League of the Ho-de-no-sau-nee, or Iroquois*, in 1851. Morgan's continuing interest in the Parker family and their welfare is revealed in a letter of recommendation included in this collection.[9]

Throughout his life, Isaac Newton Parker was both a source of pride and an embarrassment to his family. According to Arthur C. Parker, Newt Parker received a "polished education" and was a "keen student of fine literature." Nevertheless, his drinking problem "brought with it unreliability" and hindered his success in life. In the 1850s, his amorous escapades and his wanderlust proved embarrassing to his family.[10] Despite his checkered career, Parker was a keen observer of the Civil War and he served as the scribe for the Tuscarora Company.

LEWIS HENRY MORGAN
Buffalo and Erie County Historical Society

CAROLINE G. PARKER
Buffalo and Erie County Historical Society

The recipient of most of Parker's correspondence was his wife, Sara Adelaide Jemison, a teacher at the Cattaraugus Indian Reservation. Sara is the great mystery of these letters. We know too little about her, her marriage to Parker, their child Trent, and her death. We do know that they knew each other since the mid-1850s. Sara was related to Chauncey C. Jemison, a Seneca farmer and teacher as well as a Parker family friend. She was apparently more of a practicing Christian as contrasted to her less-than-observant husband. Sara was also a friend of Newt's sister Caroline while Newt was a friend of Sara's brother Tommie. Indeed, Newt's and Tommie's escapades and heavy drinking often got them into difficulty with conservative reservation residents. Tommie's "battle with the bottle" eventually led Newt to distance himself from him because Parker's family, friends, reservation folk, and missionaries were beginning to speak badly about him. Tommie's alcoholism became worse and continued to be a subject of Sara's and Newt's correspondence.[11]

In 1859, Sara and Newt started corresponding on a wide variety of subjects. In November of that year, he addressed his letter to her, *"Dear Friend Sarah."* By January 3, 1861, his letters open "My Dear and Loving Sara." After being encouraged by Martha Hoyt Parker, Newt's sister-in-law, the two were married in late February, 1861.[12] Because of their long-distance courtship and marriage—Cattaraugus and Tonawanda Indian Reservations are separated by approximately 75 miles— he kept her informed about reservation occurrences, gossiped about family and

MARTHA HOYT PARKER
Wife of Nicholson, daughter of Jonathan Hoyt
Photo taken 1896
Buffalo and Erie County Historical Society

friends, reported on personal medical concerns, and described his travels as an Indian entertainer. In contrast to Newt's schoolhouse at
Tonawanda, Sara's Cattaraugus building was less than ideal. According to
Newt, "I don't see how you manage having so many scholars in such a log
house 8 by 8 only 6 feet and a half from the floor to the upper ceiling." In
a kidding manner, he added that it was "rather a large schoolhouse for
such a small school master. I like to know where you have to stand when
all the scholars are there[.] You have to stand outdoors, don't you?"[13] On
another occasion, he referred to the hardship caused by walking six or
seven miles daily to and from his own teaching assignment on the
Tonawanda Reservation![14]

He frequently discussed reservation matters as well as his travels. Despite his family's conversion to Christianity—Newt was a Baptist—he invited his future wife to attend the Indian New Year's ceremonies at Mid-
winter at the Tonawanda Longhouse in January, 1860. She had earlier ex-
tended a similar invitation to Newt to visit ceremonies at Cattaraugus.[15] On
October 17, he told her that he was visiting the Onondaga Indian Reservation where there were plans for a "great Six Nations council" on the following day.[16] Perhaps indicative of his later interest in military service, he informed Sara, on two separate occasions, that he had served as a recording
secretary for the meeting of the "old soldiers of the War of 1812"—his
father William was a veteran—helping them draw up "papers to send to
Albany for 'state bounty' to get pay for clothing."[17] In the late winter of
1861, Newt invited her to visit Tonawanda "before the roads break up in
the Spring," an annual occurrence which still plagues the reservation.[18] By
the spring of the same year, Newt told her about the deadly progress of a
cholera epidemic which had already claimed four lives on the reservation.[19]
In the summer, he mentioned the Indians' attendance as entertainers at
the July 4th celebration in Buffalo, which to him were not so memorable
because Sara was not with him.[20] By the end of the summer of 1861, he
was reporting to her about Ick [Isaac] Doctor's numerous failed attempts
to change the Indian governmental structure at the Tonawanda Reservation, one that had been promoted by the Parker family after the ratification
of the federal Tonawanda Treaty of 1857.[21] In early 1862, he notified Sara
that he was in pursuit of a horse thief and told her about his plans to visit
the Tuscarora Reservation, about fifty miles away, in order to attend the
dedication of their new meeting house.[22] By April, he was reporting that,
while entertaining at Canandaigua Lake, he had met a Native American
couple, probably Abenaki, who were "good and kind" to him. The man
Oskinawah was apparently a chief from Lenoxville, Canada who had toured

THE OLD FARMHOUSE ON THE TONAWANDA RESERVATION
Fitted up by General Parker for his parents.

Buffalo and Erie County Historical Society

the Northeast for the last sixteen years. Newt noted that they performed before rural folk, "green as green can be," and that they "danced about half the night."[23]

Newt's letters are filled with references to medical concerns and to other annoyances. Newt wrote about his brother Levi's health, who, like Tommie Jemison, was seriously affected by alcoholism.[24] In September, 1861, Newt, who had recurring problems with his eyes, indicated for the first time of this medical problem, insisting that his eyes as well as his overall health were improving.[25] In March, 1862, while Newt was attempting to get a toothpick out of his pocket while sitting, the "sharp point came up over my nail into the flesh covering the upper part of the nail," causing him excruciating pain, making it difficult to write.[26] He was especially aggravated by the gossip of reservation residents who spread rumors of Newt's alleged amorous affairs, including one with a Penobscot woman named Elizabeth, which he had to spend time countering and explaining to his soon-to-be wife.[27]

Despite that rumor, Sara and Isaac Newton were married in the last week of February, 1861, and Newt's letters reveal a deep affection for his wife. In December of that year, their son Trent was born. After that date, we learn little about Sara from Newt's letters. We do know that Sara lived for a time in Buffalo and was in ill health, also suffering from eye problems, throughout the Civil War period. By the spring of 1864, her correspondence with her husband abruptly ends. Despite careful checking of church and cemetery records in and around the Cattaraugus Indian Reservation, tribal and museum records, and discussions with Nicholson Parker's great-granddaughter, the editor has failed to uncover the fate of Sara Adelaide Jemison Parker.[28]

Newt Parker's military service began in the late spring of 1862, after several aborted attempts to volunteer for service. The twenty-five Indians, mostly Seneca, who served in the Tuscarora Company, were mostly farmers recruited from May 12 to August 26, 1862. Newt Parker and two other Senecas—Benjamin Jonas of Cattaraugus and Henry Sundown of Tonawanda—volunteered on June 18, 1862 at Buffalo.[29] Their enlistment only occurred after the Iroquois in New York had broken down the doors to enter military service. Until the spring of 1862, the Iroquois had been repeatedly rejected for service by New York recruiters because of overt racism and because there were no laws on the books specifying the legality of Indian service since almost all Indians at that time were not United States citizens. Nevertheless, it should be noted that admitting Indians into Union service varied from locale to locale and state to state. Although Native Americans were allowed immediate entry in other areas of the North such as Pennsylvania, they were time-and-time again rejected in western New York State, as documented in Parker's October 1861 letter to Sara. Parker and other Tonawanda Seneca went to Geneseo to join Brigadier General Samuel W. Wadsworth's "Wadsworth Guards" but were discharged because they were Indians.[30] Before Parker's enlistment was rejected and he was dismissed from service for a second time, he returned to his home at Tonawanda, proudly dressed in his military uniform. As a result of war-

MUSTER ROLL

Description of Isaac Newton Parker's Enlistment

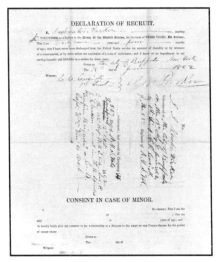

ENLISTMENT PAPERS FOR ISAAC NEWTON PARKER
Buffalo and Erie County Historical Society

time exigencies to raise additional troops to fill quotas after heavy Union battlefield losses at First Manassas and Shiloh and because of the persistent lobbying by Iroquois Indians and their non-Indian allies, local New York recruiting officers finally allowed the enlistment of Iroquois Indians by the spring of 1862.

The 132nd New York State Volunteer Infantry was known as the second regiment of the Empire or Spinola's Brigade and Hillhouse Light Infantry. It was formed in July, 1862, out of several earlier incomplete units, including the 53rd New York State Volunteer Infantry, known as the Vosburg Chasseurs and recruited by Colonel George A. Buckingham, which included those same twenty-five Iroquois Indians who were from the Allegany, Cattaraugus, Onondaga, Tonawanda, and Tuscarora Reservations; most of Company D included native born Americans and naturalized citizens of German birth recruited at Buffalo, Brooklyn, Lewiston, Manhattan, and Syracuse.[31]

Unlike African Americans, almost all Iroquois soldiers served in integrated units as officers and ordinary volunteers in the Union army and navy and received the same pay as their white counterparts. Of the twenty-five Iroquois in the Tuscarora Company, one served as corporal, two as sergeant, and one as lieutenant. Parker's writings and the letters of his white comrades in the 132nd New York State Volunteer Infantry also reveal that mutual admiration existed and male bonding occurred between Indian

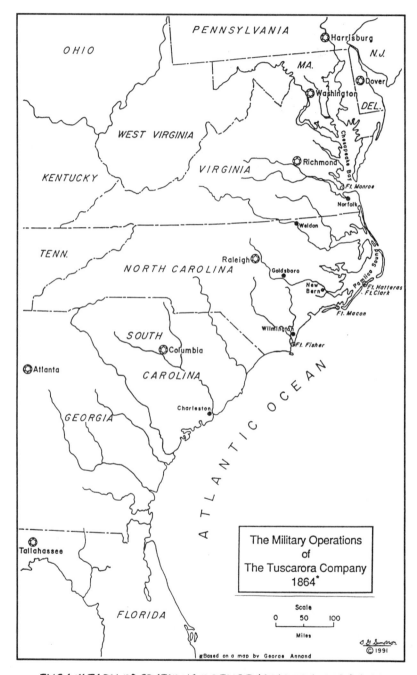

The Military Operations
of
The Tuscarora Company
1864*

Scale

0   50   100

Miles

*Based on a map by George Annand

© 1991

THE MILITARY OPERATIONS OF THE TUSCARORA COMPANY

Ben Simpson, cartographer

and non-Indian soldiers. The Iroquois soldiers were cited for meritorious service twice in the official War Department records of the Civil War. Although there was prejudice in initially denying Indian recruitment in western New York, there was little, if any, evidence of racial prejudice in the company as reflected in Parker's letters after his enlistment in June, 1862.[32]

LIEUTENANT CORNELIUS C. CUSICK

New York State Library & New York State Archives

Much of the recruitment of the Indians was done by Cornelius C. Cusick, a Tuscarora sachem. Through his lobbying efforts, the Indian troops were finally allowed to volunteer. Cusick was born on the Tuscarora Indian Reservation in western New York on August 2, 1835. His was among the most prominent families in Tuscarora history. Cusick's grandfather was Nicholas Kaghnatsho [Cusick], the bodyguard and interpreter for General Marquis de Lafayette, during the American Revolution. Because of Cusick's role in recruitment and because of his remarkable leadership of both the Indian and non-Indian troops in the unit, Company D was soon referred to as the Tuscarora Company.[33] Although there were accusations that Cusick as well as Parker profited from recruiting Iroquois soldiers for military service, no evidence of these charges has been substantiated. Later, after the Civil War, Cusick served with distinction as a captain in the regular army on the Trans-Mississippi frontier until his retirement in 1891, and subsequently, he was appointed as honorary and special assistant in the Department of American Archaeology and Ethnology at the Columbian Exposition in Chicago.[34]

Parker had several distinct reasons for enlistment in the Union army. From his childhood, he and his brothers had been inculcated with a sense of *noblesse oblige*. As an educated person, Parker had an obligation to serve his community with the skills he had acquired in the white man's world. Going off to war also satisfied Newt's own personality quirks such as his lifelong wanderlust. As a man frequently faced with debt, Civil War military service allowed him to make a steady but small income. Perhaps most importantly, the war also offered him a way to follow in his father's foot-

| Name | Rank | Age | Height | Occupation | Joined for Duty and Enrolled | | | Term | Discharge |
					When	Where	By Whom Enrolled		
Bailey, Smith	pvt.	23	5'5"	farmer	7/22/1862	Buffalo	C. C. Cusick	3 years	6/29/1865
Cusick, Cornelius C.	lieut.	27	5'7"	farmer	5/12/1862	New York City	Col. Buckingham	3 years	6/29/1865
Garlow, George	pvt.	32	5'7'	farmer/musician	5/31/1862	Lewiston	C. C. Cusick	3 years	5/25/1865
Green, Edward	pvt.	23	5'5"	farmer	6/28/1862	Buffalo	C. C. Cusick	3 years	Disability discharge 9/15/1863
Halfwhite, James	pvt.	25	5'9"	farmer	5/24/1862	Cattaraugus	C. C. Jemison	3 years	5/25/1865
Hudson, Foster	sgt.	23	5'7"	farmer	5/24/1862	Cattaraugus	C. C. Jemison	3 years	Shot Jackson Mills, NC; died
Isaacs, Samuel G.	pvt.	26	6'1"	farmer	5/24/1862	Cattaraugus	C. C. Jemison	3 years	5/25/1865
Jacobs, Hewlitt	pvt.	20	5'6"	farmer	5/31/1862	Lewiston	C. C. Cusick	3 years	5/25/1865
Jameson, Cyrus	cpl.	27	5'10"	farmer	6/24/1862	Buffalo	C. C. Cusick	3 years	Transf. to U.S. Navy
Jameson, George W.	pvt.	23	6'1"	farmer	5/24/1862	Cattaraugus	C. C. Jemison	3 years	5/25/1865
Jameson, Jesse	pvt.	22	5'8"	farmer	7/22/1862	Buffalo	C. C. Cusick	3 years	6/29/1865
Jonas, Benjamin	pvt.	27	5'9"	farmer	6/18/1862	Buffalo	C. C. Cusick	3 years	6/29/1865
Kennedy, William	pvt.	19	5'4"	farmer	7/16/1862	Buffalo	C. C. Cusick	3 years	Died at Andersonville Prison of scorbatus 9/27/1864
Mason, William	pvt.	18	5'3"	farmer	6/13/1862	Tonawanda	C. C. Cusick	3 years	6/29/1865
Moore, Charles	pvt.	35	6'2"	farmer	6/13/1862	Cattaraugus	C. C. Cusick	3 years	6/29/1865
Parker, Isaac Newton	sgt.	29	5'8"	farmer	6/18/1862	Buffalo	C. C. Cusick	3 years	6/29/1865
Peters, Jeremiah (Jerry)	pvt.	21	5'7"	farmer	6/1/1862	Lewiston	C. C. Cusick	3 years	—
Peters, John	pvt.	22	5'3"	farmer	5/31/1862	Buffalo	C. C. Cusick	3 years	5/25/1865
Powles, Abram	cpl.	26	5'9"	farmer	8/26/1862	New York City	Capt. A. W. Smith	3 years	6/29/1865
Redeye, Martin	pvt.	25	5'8"	carpenter	7/22/1862	Buffalo	C. C. Cusick	3 years	Disability discharge 3/26/1863
Snow, George	pvt.	32	6'	farmer	5/24/1862	Cattaraugus	C. C. Jemison	3 years	5/25/1865
Sundown, Henry	pvt.	24	5'8"	farmer	6/18/1862	Buffalo	C. C. Cusick	3 years	6/29/1865
Titus, John	pvt.	22	5'9"	farmer	7/22/1862	Buffalo	C. C. Cusick	3 years	6/29/1865
Warmee, Jacob	pvt.	38	6'	farmer	5/24/1862	Cattaraugus	C. C. Jemison	3 years	5/25/1865
Wilson, George	pvt.	34	5'10"	farmer	5/24/1862	Cattaraugus	C. C. Jemison	3 years	5/25/1862

CHART OF D COMPANY, 132 NYS VOL. INFANTRY:
The Iroquois Indians of the Tuscarora Company
(compiled from Descriptive Muster Rolls, NA and NYSA, and Iroquois community records)

steps, as a warrior in mortal combat, a time-honored route to influence and status among his Seneca people. Perhaps more importantly, the Tonawanda Seneca's white attorney, Brigadier General John Martindale, played a major role in the Union war effort, a fact not lost on Parker or the other Indians of Company D.

The Iroquois troops were transferred into the 132nd New York State Volunteer Infantry when the 53rd New York State Volunteer Infantry, a fancy-dressed Zouave regiment, was disbanded in the summer of 1862. After receiving assurances of getting a $25 bounty, a $2 premium, and a month's pay of $13 for enlisting, the twenty-five

BRIGADIER GENERAL
JOHN H. MARTINDALE
National Archives, III Photo B-4083

Indians were sent to Camp Scrogg in New York City. There they trained on the parade grounds and received regimental inspection.[35] On September 28, 1862, the regiment was sent to Washington, D.C., and temporarily camped adjacent to the Capitol. A week later, the Indians were mustered into federal service for three years and sent to Suffolk, Virginia for reconnoitering, constructing works of defense, and outpost duty at Camp Hoffman at Fort Monroe under Major General John Peck of Syracuse, New York.[36]

On Christmas eve, 1862, the unit was transferred to New Bern, North Carolina, which had been captured by Major General Ambrose Burnside in March of that year. Ironically, the Iroquois soldiers found themselves in the precise area that the Tuscarora had been removed from one hundred and fifty years earlier. In fact, one of the towns in the environs of New Bern is named Tuscarora. They were now assigned to guard the railways and prevent the Confederacy from resupplying its forces by sea. Commanded by Colonel Peter J. Claassen, a non-Indian, the regiment was attached to the 2nd Brigade, 5th Division, 18th Army Corps to July, 1863; on outpost duty, at Batchelder's Creek near New Bern from May, 1863; in Palmer's Brigade, Peck's Division, 18th Army Corps, from January, 1864; in the Department of Virginia and North Carolina from April, 1864; in the Provisional Corps, North Carolina from March 1, 1865; in the 1st Brigade, 2nd Division, 23rd Army Corps from April 2, 1865; at Salisbury, North Carolina from May, 1865 until its being relieved of its duties and transferred to New York City, where it was honorably mustered out of Union military service on June 29, 1865. The following is a summary of the 132nd New York State Volunteer Infantry's military actions—battles, engagements, and skirmishes:[37]

1862:
October: Engagement at Blackwater, Va.
November: Skirmish at Franklin, Va., Zuni, Va.

1863:
March 4: Skirmish at Pollocksville, N.C.
March 6: Skirmish at Trenton, N.C.
March 14: Attack on and defense of New Bern, N.C.
April 9: Action at Blount's Creek and at the following: Swift Creek, Blount's Mills, Blount's Ridge, New Hope Church School House, N.C.
April 16: Skirmish at Sandy Ridge, N.C.
April 20: Skirmish at Sandy Ridge or Loard's Creek, N.C.
May 23: Engagement at Batchelder's Creek, N.C.

1864:
February 1: Engagement at Batchelder's Creek, near New Bern and Cobbs Creek, N.C.; cited for Heroic defense of bridge and block-house.
February 1-4: Engagement at New Bern, N.C.
June 21: Surprise and capture of Interior Grand Guard at Jackson's Mills, N.C. near S.W. Creek dam.
June 22: Engagement with Exterior Grand Guard at Jackson's Mills.
December 9: Action at Gardner's Bridge, new Plymouth, N.C.
December 10: Skirmish at Foster's Mills, N.C.
December 11-12: Action, attack, and capture of enemies' bridge-head, and redan; colors planted by Color Sergeant Isaac N. Parker at Butler's Bridge, Southwest Creek, N.C.

1865:
March 1: Campaign of the Carolinas.
March 8-9-10: Battle at Wise's Forks, N.C. near Jackson's Mills and Kinston, N.C.; Campaign of the Carolinas.
March 29-31: Skirmish at Snow Hill, N.C.; Campaign of the Carolinas.
April: Escort, to General William Tecumseh Sherman's supply wagon train from Goldsboro, N.C. to Kinston, N.C. and return; Campaign of the Carolinas.
April 26: The surrender of General Joseph E. Johnston at Bennett House, Durham Station, N.C.

In his three-year service in the regiment, Parker worked in a variety of positions. First, he was assigned to headquarters, working as a clerk. He then was made an orderly sergeant and served in camp duty. Subsequently, he was assigned to the signal corps. Finally he was made color bearer, which placed him in harm's way because the Confederate forces always attempted to shoot the color bearer to slow Union advance. Despite the tremendous risk of serving in this capacity, Parker survived and was cited for his role in this position in December, 1864.[38]

Camp life of the 132nd in North Carolina included parade drills, forced marches through ankle-deep mud, and delayed wages. At times, work details relieved some of the anxiety and monotony of army life. Despite these negative aspects of camp life, there were also more pleasant sides as well. The camp had a bowling alley and theatre. Moreover, the general anxiety about the war was broken by parties and by entertainment. Whiskey rations, an "army gallon," were dispensed to the troops. Parker also reported the visit of black singers or minstrels. On another occasion, the troops came together honoring their white captain, Thomas Green, on his birthday with a party and the presentation of a gold watch. The letters once again reveal that the soldiers, Indian and non-Indian, bonded together in the face of death that surrounded them.[39]

Parker's letter to his sister-in-law on April 1, 1864 reveals his deep feelings about his comrades-in-arms. At the Battle of Batchelder's Creek in February, 1864, Parker reflected on the gruesome death of First Lieutenant Arnold Zenette, a non-Indian and the quartermaster of the Tuscarora Company, which he described in grisly detail. Zenette was attempting to supply ammunition to men in the entrenchments. According to Parker, the quartermaster was first captured, then robbed, and finally tortured to death by Confederate soldiers.[40]

In all, the regiment lost one officer and six enlisted men in combat; seven enlisted men and one officer died of disease and other causes; and seventy-one enlisted men died as prisoners of war. At least twenty-eight enlisted died when torpedo mines stored at Batchelder's Creek, North Carolina accidentally exploded on May 26, 1864. As for the Iroquois Indians in the regiment, one Indian, Sergeant Foster J. Hudson, a Seneca, was killed in action; another Seneca, Private William Kennedy, died as a prisoner at Andersonville. Although no Indian casualties occurred during the torpedo accident, Parker was, nevertheless, thrown fifty feet into the air by the explosion.[41]

Corresponding with his wife as well as receiving mail from home brought temporary relief from these fears. They also brought with them other concerns. Kept in the dark by military supervisors and isolated from the news on other fronts of the war, Parker told his wife on February 3, 1863, that she probably knew more about what was happening in the war than he did. When bounty agents began to conscript underage Seneca recruits for military service and when some Iroquois recruits were not paid their promised bounties, Parker was informed of these doings. News from home brought other problems and weighed on Parker heavily. He was especially concerned by his parents' failing health and his inability to be granted a furlough to visit home. Only after his father died in the Spring of 1863 did Parker receive a furlough which he used to attend the funeral. Equally vexing was his separation from his wife Sara. As the war continued, their relationship was increasingly strained, with Newt frequently disturbed about her failure to write to him.[42]

Parker had other pressing concerns. Army life required preciseness and Parker's valued imported German watch was in disrepair in 1863. His fears of not having a proper working timepiece made him send the watch for fixing to his wife in Buffalo, because to him North Carolinian watch repairers were unreliable and less able than those found in the North.[43] Despite this low estimation of southern artisanry, Parker did not view all North Carolinians with the same disdain. He fought side by side with North Carolinian Unionists. He also differentiated enemy Confederates from the general populace of the South. Enemy "rebs" were capable of any atrocity.[44] On the other hand, local North Carolinians were viewed as thoughtful friendly people who served the Union army's needs, as cooks, seamstresses, and grocers. In June, 1864, Parker asked his sister to send him his moccasins to relieve the suffering from his "heavy government shoes" that were "unbearable" during the hot summer months. He also asked her to send him two Iroquois pudding sticks and two ladles, which he planned to give as presents to two local Southern families who had provided him meals, a welcome relief from army rations.[45]

By the fall of 1863, Parker's enthusiasm for military service had cooled. When one Indian returned from furlough and brought news from the Cattaraugus Reservation, Parker's changed attitude was clearly revealed. Parker's sister Caroline incorrectly informed him that one Indian named Ed Green had reenlisted for military service after being discharged because of a persistent dry cough. Parker reacted by labeling Green a "Great Fool" who had reenlisted "for money I reckon."[46] After being promoted to "Sergeant Color Bearer" on December 20, 1863 and once again receiving letters from his wife, Newt rebounded and his spirits were, at least temporarily, raised.[47] His later attempts to secure a commission as captain failed, despite a personal recommendation by the anthropologist Morgan about Parker's character and leadership qualities, which Morgan forwarded to General Butler.[48]

In early January, 1864, General Robert E. Lee recommended to Jefferson Davis an attack on the Union army at New Bern in order to capture the large amounts of provisions there. Lee was also intent on recapturing the railroad at New Bern, which had been guarded by the Tuscarora Company and other Union forces since 1862; however, Lee badly underestimated his enemy's abilities and Davis chose the wrong commander, Major General George E. Pickett, to lead the strike.

Pickett, who had been sent to the Department of Virginia and North Carolina to recuperate and recruit after the disaster at Gettysburg, had approximately 13,000 troops under his command. They included brigades commanded by Brigadier Generals Seth M. Barton, Thomas L. Clingman, Montgomery D. Corse, Robert F. Hoke and Matthew Ransom. With Pickett were also Colonel John N. Whitford's 67th North Carolina; Colonel James Dearing's column of the 15th and 17th Virginia, two or three regiments of Confeder-

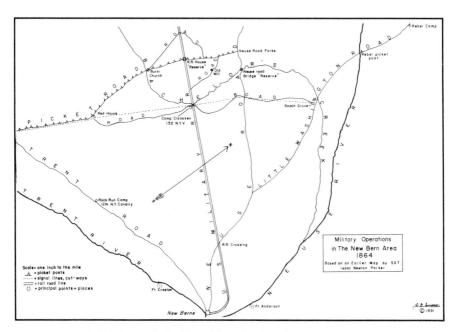

MILITARY OPERATIONS IN THE NEW BERN AREA

based on an original map by Sergeant Isaac Newton Parker in a letter of February 1, 1864 in the American Philosophical Society

Ben Simpson, cartographer, and the American Philosophical Society

MAJOR GENERAL GEORGE PICKETT (C.S.A.)

National Archives, III Photo BA-1191

ate Cavalry, including the 3rd North Carolina Cavalry. This expedition also included fourteen Confederate naval cutters under Commander James Taylor Wood's direction.

General Pickett moved on New Bern on January 30, 1864, dividing his troops into three columns. Barton and his men were to cross the Trent River near Trenton and proceed to the south side of the river to Brice's Creek below New Bern. He was to take the forts along the Neuse and Trent rivers and then enter New Bern via the railroad bridge, thus preventing Union reinforcement by land or water. Colonels Dearing and Whitford and their men were to move down the Neuse River and capture Fort Anderson. Hoke and Pickett and the remainder of the expeditionary force were to "move down between the Trent and the Neuse, endeavor to surprise the troops on Batchelder's Creek, silence the guns in the star fort and batteries near the Neuse, and penetrate the town in that direction." The Confederate navy was to descend the Neuse, capture Union gunboats, and cooperate with the three Confederate columns.[49]

Pickett "bungled the New Bern operations," although he shifted blame to Generals Barton and Hoke. Pickett had failed in planning beforehand, underestimating, as Lee did, the task at hand. General Hoke moved quickly to reach Batchelder's Creek before Union forces could destroy the bridge there, but the firing of pickets had warned the garrison of the enemy's approach. The troops then destroyed the bridge to prevent the Confederates' advance. Hoke also failed to capture the Union train and was unable to enter the city by rail. Neverthe-

BRIGADIER GENERAL SETH BARTON (C.S.A.)

National Archives, III Photo BA-1840

MAJOR GENERAL ROBERT F. HOKE (C.S.A.)

Promoted to that grade
April 20, 1864
National Archives, III Photo BA-1205

less, Hoke's men adapted to the circumstances and cut down trees which two of Hoke's regiments used to cross the creek. Despite Union reinforcements, Hoke routed them once his troops crossed Batchelder's Creek. His men then marched to within a mile of New Bern waiting to join Barton's forces.[50]

Barton never reached Hoke. After passing through low swamp country with vast mud holes caused by winter showers, Barton came in view of the enemy's breastworks close to Brice's Creek at 8:00 A.M. on February 1. Instead of attacking immediately, which might have caught the Union forces by surprise, Barton, along with General Ransom and Colonel William R. Aylett, made a reconnaissance while bringing up his artillery. The reconnaissance found that the 99th and 132nd New York State Volunteers were more entrenched than previously thought. Barton concluded, and then reported to General Pickett, that his troops were "unprepared to encounter so serious" and "insurmountable" a defense. In the meantime, the Union artillery began to hit Barton's position. Pickett then ordered Barton to join the troops before New Bern for an assault on that front. Yet to do so, Barton had to cross the Trent River and retrace his steps, which would have taken more than two days. When Pickett learned that Barton and his men could not reach him until February 4, Pickett withdrew on February 3 and admitted failure. Although the Union suffered more than twice as many casualties—one hundred compared to the Confederate forty-five—the Confederates failed to capture the supplies they so desperately needed and sought.[51]

During the engagement, the 99th and 132nd New York State Volunteers and 12th New York State Cavalry, as well as the 1st and 2nd North Carolina Union Infantry faced this Confederate onslaught. Under Claassen's command, the Union forces in Company D held their ground until the Confederates brought up their artillery pieces. The Indians were part of the Union picket post holding access to Batchelder's Creek on the Neuse Road Bridge and at an old mill near the railroad. They did so until overcome by overwhelming Confederate numbers. Claassen, as did Generals

Butler and Peck, later cited the Indians of the Tuscarora Company for hero-
ism in the official record.[52] Captain Charles G. Smith, the General Officer
of the Day (February 10, 1864) of the 132nd New York State Volunteer
Infantry, commended Cusick and several other commanders at Batchelder's
Creek for their "individual instances of coolness and heroism." After laud-
ing one "Lieutenant Haring" for his bravery in defending the Neuse bridge,
Smith added: "In this he [Haring] was nobly seconded by Capt. Thomas B.
Green, Lieutenant Cusick, and Companies D and G, with Lieutenants Gear-
ing & Ryan, who were both badly wounded, the respective companies los-
ing heavily."[53] Later, Captain R. Emmett Fiske, also of the New York State
Volunteer Infantry, wrote of the fight at Batchelder's Creek: "Lieutenant
Cusick with some thirty of his warrior soldiers of his tribe, engaged the
rebel advance in a sharp skirmish for several hours and by desperate fighting prevented the dislodgement of the picket reserves and the capture of
the outpost camp."[54]

That bloody skirmish was later described by Parker in shorthand fash-
ion. The Seneca sergeant wrote about the swampy terrain, made a map of
the battlefield, and mentioned the capture of Private William Kennedy, a
Seneca Indian, who was sent to Andersonville Prison where he later died.
Indeed, the regiment paid a costly price. The 132nd New York lost five
men, six others were wounded, while eighty were captured.[55]

In June of 1864, the remaining members of the regiment were sent on
a forced march — seventy-three miles in thirty-nine hours — to the vicinity
of Kinston, North Carolina. While on reconnaissance at Jackson's Mills,
Lieutenant Cusick, "leading his Indians in a flank movement, distinguished
himself by materially assisting in the capture of the commandant of Kinston,
N.C. ... together with five of his officers and upwards of fifty of his rank &
file." They also captured fifty-one other Confederate soldiers and inflicted
thirty to forty casualties. Captain Thomas B. Green, his officers and men
were cited in the official record for the success of the operation which was
attributed to their "endurance and determination."[56] Claassen later wrote
that at Jackson's Mills, North Carolina, Cusick and his "dusky warriors"
lying in wait in a "roadside thicket, with instructions to closely guard the
rear," completely trapped the rebels.[57]

After the engagement at Jackson's Mills, Newt Parker's correspondence to his family ends. The Tuscarora Company's last major encounter
with Confederate forces occurred on March 7-10, 1865, at Wise's Forks,
(also known as the Battle of Kinston), North Carolina. There Major General Jacob Dolson Cox's two divisions of the XXIII Corps fought with
General Braxton Bragg's forces under Major Generals Robert F. Hoke

REVEREND ASHER WRIGHT
Buffalo and Erie County Historical Society

and D. H. Hill. One of the casualties at the skirmish was Foster J. Hudson, 7th Sergeant of the company and a Seneca Indian from the Cattaraugus Reservation. Once again Parker was the conveyor of the bad news to his fellow Seneca. In a letter to Asher Wright, the well-respected Presbyterian missionary to the Seneca, he graphically described Hudson's death. On March 7, 1865, his Seneca comrade had been shot in the left knee joint at Jackson's Mills, North Carolina. After falling with his wounds, Confederate soldiers robbed him of his watch. D Company liberated him, and he was then sent to the military hospital at New Bern, since the bullet was lodged deep in the joint. Subsequently, surgeons there amputated his leg. Although there were hopes of recovery, Hudson died on March 23 of a hemorrhage just seventeen days before the end of the Civil War.[58]

Parker and eight other Indian comrades of the Tuscarora Company were mustered out of service on June 29, 1865. Benjamin Jonas and Henry Sundown, who had volunteered with Parker at Buffalo on the same day in 1862, left service with him.[59] On December 31, 1866, Lewis Henry Morgan, once again serving as Parker's patron, recommended the Seneca for a commission as a second lieutenant in the United States Army, writing to Congressman Burton C. Cook of Illinois: "In October last I wrote to Lieu. Gen. Sherman, asking him if he would take Isaac N. Parker into the Military Service, in his District, and in due time have him promoted with a commission in the regular Army if he deserved it." Morgan added: "Mr. Parker is a Seneca Indian the youngest brother of Colonel Ely S. Parker of Genl. Grants staff, and the equal of his brother in capacity." Two months earlier, Morgan had sent a similar recommendation to Secretary of War Edwin M. Stanton. On September 18, 1867, Stanton granted the request for a commission and Parker was commissioned a second lieutenant in the 36th United States Infantry. Unfortunately, Parker's military career ended soon after when he failed to pass the army's physical examination because of his poor eyesight.[61]

Parker's later life is impossible to reconstruct. The few surviving records indicate that he frequently sought out his brother Ely's help for employment or a special favor. Moreover, he challenged the power of the Tonawanda Council of Chiefs for some unknown reason and soon found himself out of favor on the reservation. Parker went west as a teacher. During Reconstruction, he married a Cherokee in Indian Territory. Her identity remains unknown.[62] According to Arthur C. Parker, Newt, in his last years, worked in Montana "where he contracted a fatal malady. He fell dead from his horse as he journeyed over the prairie and was buried on the plains near the spot where he died."[63]

THE LETTERS

Recruitment

National Hotel
Oct 9th 1861
Buffalo
Wednesday afternoon

Affectionate Dear—
Glory to <u>God</u>!!! I. N. Parker is not accepted in the volunteers service for the "U.S. Army". The officer of the "Mustering Office of the U.S. Office" could not accept <u>me</u> because there is no regulation, that is no law for accepting the "red man" in "U.S." law on the subject. So my Dear Sara it is all right aint it—now! [–]—I will write in full in my next, it is now 2:00 p.m., and in great haste too.—2:30 bound for Corfu.—I'll try to see you in a few days—after the Indian Agt comes to Tonawanda. Love & Kisses to my Dear Sweet Sara.

From Your Dear <u>Newt</u>

Got back this morning from Catt[araugus], no ann[uity] till next Tues[day]—

Newt

P.S. Enclosed some stamps write soon—train time

Your Newt

[ALS, INP, BECHS]

At home, Nov. 12th 1861
9 A.M.

My Dear Wife—
    I wrote a short letter to you on yesterday afternoon but it wont go until
12 o'clock today noon for Batavia way.—and this can't go until I start back
for the seat of war, Geneseo. I had thought that, I with a couple of others,
would go back on the night or tomorrow early. But now I guess that we
wont go back until Thursday night or friday morning. To be there some
time on friday, so as to do the organizing on Saturday. So I'll mail this at
East Pembroke or Batavia on our way out. I'm wade in so awful muddy in
these diggings that it is easier for a lazy fellow like me to go afloat. So I did
on yesterday afternoon. I went to the Centre [–] start down through the
woods and came back by the same road way. The way that we came here
when you was here. I suppose you remember the road to the Centre, direct
from there to here. You know that I wrote that I got home about 11 o'clock
a.m. of yesterday. Just as I got home I saw the [–] hitched up to the demo-
crat wagon— I [–] and found Carrie [Caroline Parker] and Ely [Ely S.
Parker] all ready for a start. I asked if he was. (or they.) going to Alabama.
No was the answer. We are going to Alabama Batavia, says Ely. So I said
nothing more— They are coming back some time today, I suppose— I was
going on a tramp of some 8 or 10 miles today but I was or am now so tired
that I guess I wont go today, but will try to go on tomorrow if I am well. I
could but just make out to get down stairs this morning. I was so awful sore
in my muscles of my understanding. do you know what they are, have you
got any [–] answer: maybe you have. you probably might [–] know – aint it
dear? By the [way]— Chauce [Chauncey C. Jemison] has not answered my
letter— I wonder what the reason is? [He] Backed out or is it Addie's fault
or what is it—
    —when I go to Catt[araugus Indian Reservation] I will go in my sol-
diers uniform— Won't the injuns look— I guess they wont get-out. I will
let you know in time when I am about to go— Your Newt. No news of any
importance as I have heard since my return. I would like to see your cousin
H. E. [Hattie] Twoguns just for greens, and in what she would have to say
for her self.[1] I was here at Tonawanda a week ago last Sunday. I did not
come to our home but right to the Meeting House church in my soldiers
uniform. [I] got there about 2:30 in the afternoon— Elder Warran was
about half[way] through preaching. Every body lunged out their eyes to
see me dressed so. Your cousin for one. I did not get a chance to speak to
her. She slip[p]ed out and went home—and I now dont doubt a bit that she

has written letters to Catt[araugus] telling some awful things about your good Newt. about my [being] dressed in soldiers clothes, and coming to church in that dress—some thing new for the Injuns, I expect, to see an Indian dressed in soldier's uniform— Would it be for my sweet dear! No I guess not for you saw a chance to see so many in the City [Buffalo], of all kinds of soldiers uniforms— Aint it Sara?— No doubt that she has written my cousin [–]—telling her all about Newton, how he was dressed, how he looked etc, etc and so on pigs tail— There is a story around here bout—, that say, I am getting Indians to enlist in the war, and when I get them in Geneseo I draw so much per head and when I get all I possibly can, then I am [–] I can [– –] and mind my own business—and let the Injun soldiers go to the dance. I guess that they trust [–] [Cornelius C.] Cusick [–] so: I should be the first one shot then [–] in action—aint it so—dear. Nine men [–] of us sworn in to gather at one time and the [ ] boys can tell for themselves—if there is any thing [ ] of that kind. I am willing to be investigated, put under arrest, if they saw fit. I am not abit [a bit] afraid in the least— I suppose that you aint playing up old man this week now are you? Having got back from Allegany [Indian Reservation]— Tell me in your next [letter] of their luck— Me showing your letters? No never! I never have as yet and [–] that intend very soon—who has better than to believe it[;] only you wanted to ask me for fun to see what I would say—aint that so my dear?— Well I must now close for the present for maybe I can't fill it some time tomorrow— Hattie is teaching, commenced yesterday— Carrie [Caroline Parker] commences on next monday in the school that I taught last winter. Love and a sweet kiss to my dearest Sara— From Your Own Dear Newt.—

P.S. Thursday Noon, 11th Nov[.] 1861. My nephew, Levi's boy, is going down to [– –] Geneseo on tomorrow (friday) morning or evening so as to be there on saturday morning— I have a letter in Geneseo nearly finished that I will send to you when I get back—6 pages of this size sheet. a great deal, aint it? [–] getting to read it for it will take you half a day to read it— I will see you on Christmas or New Years, if I am well.—if I have to go [a]foot to Buffalo, I mean [–]—for if I am well, I of course can make it—so he alooking out—keep waiting as usual to here until I tell you different— For they [are] all safe here if I am sent [it] here for a few days— I will be back here quite often as long as we will be in Geneseo— I may go to Catt[araugus] for more injun soldiers by and by— I calculate to any law— write soon—

Love and kiss to my wife—
From your Husband
I. N. Parker

I saw a great many girls yesterday—who hates Hatt [Hattie] awfully - for they says, she is to[o] overbearing in her remarks about folks—of course that aint right, is it <u>dear</u>?— To abuse people for nothing <u>less tongue</u> and <u>more thinking</u> is sometimes the best policy, aint it Dear?— Let that be <u>ours</u> is the wish of

Your Newt

[ALS, INP, BECHS]

Nov. 19, 1861
Alabama Nov. 19th 1861

Beloved Wife—

How I do love to occupy my spare moments in writing to my own good
<u>Dear</u>, not only to make up [for] lost time, no not at all. For in fact, I have
been so busy—and part of the time while at Geneseo I hadn't my writing
materials with me, consequently I thus could not write. and when I got my
writing materials there, then the case was that I expected daily to come
home. I went out on Monday, and I expected just as sure as I was a living
man, that I would return on the very next (tuesday) day. But it was tomorrow and tomorrow and so it went until Sunday morning, when I at last was
decided that <u>I</u> would go home any how, let the consequences be what they
may— So I started— I got home as I have already told you in my former
letter—aint it Dear? You asked me "how I felt and how the state of my
mind is"— Well <u>dear</u>, I feel in better health quite well. I cannot now com-
plain of my stay in Geneseo all winter. I will surely get fat and I am afraid
quite <u>fussey</u> and double chin all together. then, what will you think of your
Newty. In the state of my mind. In mind I feel quite comfortable—when I
think of <u>you</u>. think of you as being my dear. I feel consoled I feel glad —
and I feel happy to know that I have one in this world who does <u>love</u> me
truly and dearly, and to whom I can fly, in whose arms I can rest with care,
when I may return from the awful seat of <u>war</u>—also that my wife as well as
my aged mother, have consoled themselves to let Newton go to <u>war</u> and to
let him have out his war fever— I honor you both for the privilage and it is
and shall ever be my sincere prayer to our kind <u>God</u> to spare our lives and
to protect us, and permit us all to [ ] meet again— Especially <u>you</u> [ ] my
own <u>Dear</u> and beloved wife. <u>God</u> has been the means of bringing in <u>you</u>
and <u>I</u> together. It is <u>Him</u>, <u>who</u> has joined us together— It is <u>Him</u>, <u>Who</u> has
directed my steps towards the battle field—as we now suppose. It is <u>Him</u>,
<u>who</u> will take care of <u>you</u> and <u>I</u> to keep us in the land of the living— Oh my
Dear. Let us both ever be trying in our daily walks, to be as good as we can
towards <u>Him</u>, and with <u>His</u> help may we grow better and at last may we be
able to serve <u>Him</u> and to live for <u>Him</u>— My Dear Remember the words of
your <u>dear</u> and beloved husband.—now bound for the <u>war</u>— Love and Kisses
to Sara

From Your Own Newt.

P.S. The council is in full blast [–] quite a number from abroad Canada Onondaga [Six Nations Reserve]— Jake Scanandoah for one—and lots from Catt.[araugus]— Expect; to [–] on tomorrow night— I have to act as Assistant Marshal to Ed Poodry—also a white man. dont know when we will go back to Geneseo— Write soon Dear— Love and Kisses Sara.

> From your loving husband
> Newt

I'll give you the particulars in my next [letter] of the council— I have called at the school of your cousin Hatt[ie] Twoguns—appeared scared seeing me in my soldiers uniform[.] Would it scare you dear—no I guess not

> Newt

[ALS, INP, BECHS]

At home, Parker St. No. 2
Jan[uar]y 13th 1862

My Beloved Wife—
Your loving letter has duly reached me and [the] contents [have] been several times read over, the arrival of which I have already told you— I see nothing special in your dear letter that I think requires answering— Only that, I am happy indeed to learn that you were well and have been and is yet enjoying [–] "tip-top" [–] with— But be assured on this: that I am happy and enjoying [–]— It is always quite refreshing [–] my mind to know of you in person [– –] generally at the time of writing— Although I do really wish some time that you would try one and while to write a real good long letter—and I will also try the same [– – –] as I can—will you try <u>dear</u>? My calculation has been and is yet to go up to Catt[araugus Indian Reservation] on a week from this saturday, and stay only one sunday and come back on Monday— I cant stand it to stay away any longer than that, for it is always an awful lonesome there up to Mr. [Asher] Wrights now and next week on thursday or maybe before—and I will try to write on Tuesday or Wednesday of next week so I will be at the office on friday or saturday of the same week— I think some of going is my <u>injun</u> when I go just out of curiosity for the "[–]" of Catt[araugus]— Nic [Nicholson Parker] saw me in my uniform when he was [–] here— I have [–] you my calculation, but I am daily expecting [– –] in Geneseo which may demand my immediate [–] there, as maybe I or you will have in Catt[araugus] [–] with the <u>Col</u>[onel] of the [–] detail of Volunteers at Geneseo— We talk of [– –] for our pay, and some other things which I aint [–] here to relate, but will defer it till we meet etc.—at present we only have our uniforms, for our pay as we may call it [ ] besides the board that we had while there— The average dues of nine buys for seven weeks ought to be some where in the neighborhood of $22.00 a piece—while [my] service ought to be about from 26 to $28.00 because I had the "Sergeantship" the latter part of my time, which would make [–] alittle more than the rest— I am now corresponding with a lawyer upon the subject. How we shall determine remains for him to decide— I hear that brother Chauce [Chauncey C. Jemison] is playing the foul game in his operation of enlisting men.— I suppose that if <u>I</u> wanted to be mean[,] I could throw Chauce higher than a <u>kite</u>—I make no [–] for such is lucky the [–]— I [– –] aint no business with the <u>War</u> matters any how. But I have no such disposition to cut up any such mean caper with Chauce or any one else— Chauce will find out for himself by and by—aint it <u>dear</u>? I guess so— I say again that a great many things. I will have to tell you when we

meet in person that I cant now on paper and in some way and occasionally pass some insinuations to me upon you—my dear <u>wife</u>— I dont generally say much, only thinking to myself that she has a whole life time to satisfy herself in.— In which case I think she will [–] afore long.— I will tell you the particulars when I am out. Our commissioner of our schools (a white man.) did not want Hattie to come on acc[ount] of the reputation she was beginning to have there up to Catt[araugus] about her dancing Indian dance etc.— She is having a full school considering the story about her.— Says she wants to go home most awfully [be]cause; [her] sister Jennie has a "pappoose" be[cause] says that [– – –] no giving one in the family for some 13 or 14 years— How is it in your family?— Would they like their Sara for [– –] a [–]? or is there enough in the family for [– –] having any? I rather think so—and more than that, I wouldn't want a [–] our just to please other people—would you dear? We have so much to do in the family that I must now teach this and next week for Carrie [Caroline Parker]—butcher hogs next week— Oh dear me! It makes me all of impatience. I want to see you so bad. <u>Dear</u> [– – –]—

From Your Beloved
Newt

[ALS, INP, BECHS]

At home. No. 7 Parker St.
Ton[awanda] Res[ervation]
Sat[urday] Dec. 28, 1861

My Beloved Dear—
    Good news for you, for over the hill and valley of Geneseo— I together
with the rest of my Indian boys are completely and totally discouraged
from the service of the United States or from this States services by the
Excellency and Commander–in–Chief and Major General of the forces of
the State of New York, the governor [Governor] E. D. Morgan.[2] The Special Code No. [–] was issued from Albany on the 23rd instant by the Adj't
Gen'l Tho[ma]s;. Hillhouse.— The main order was sent direct [to] Geneseo
and I got the copy on yesterday— I was going back to Geneseo on yesterday, got [– – – – –] heard that [– –] had arrived. I then traveled and came
back— Long toward evening it began to rain. at midnight it began to [–] a
complete hurricane—and in the morning I gave up going out maybe Monday [– –] health [– –] permitting.— You see that I just go back there and
get my things. I have a large bag full out there, and, [–] see if we are going
to be paid or not, and whether they'll want to take; the uniforms from us
or not— Write hereafter to Alabama [New York] as usual etc. I'll write
again about [– –] you may be at home long looked for Trent as that you
can hit him, him[,] hugg him[,] choke him, clasp him and last[,] all or
most of all give him a sweet-lovely kiss.[3]— [–] it Dear?— I [– –] in [–]
hoping that [– – –] health. The time is for kisses for Sara
                                        [– – –] Newt

[– – –] Tuesday

My Sara
    [– – – – –] day it is Dear—inst: you [have] a happy New Year— I am not
very well so had to send a man to Geneseo this morning at 2 o'clock— I
expect that you will be in Buffalo at this time—it will be just like it—aint it
dear? Don't write any more to Geneseo— But to here—hope you are well—
Love and a kiss to Sara.
                                        Your Newt

[ALS, INP, BECHS]

At home. Febr[uar]y 23rd, 1862
Sunday 5 a.m.

Dear Wife[,]

I write to you at <u>this</u> home of our Lord's holy Day with a deep and sorrowful heart. Your dear Newt is bereaved of a fond affectionate and a <u>dear Mother</u>. My aged Mother, your later Mother-in-law departed this life at half past five o'clock this morning—after a severe and long illness—<u>only</u> two days and two nights.— The chill of a cold setting and causing the inflamation of the bowel, made thereby mortification settling in which ended her Indian's life. God in his altruism and providence has seen it to remove <u>us</u> of a <u>Mother</u>, and to take her, as far [–] from this sinful world to a better and happier world beyond the [–] Oh! I pray <u>to not</u> let me think that <u>God</u> has been cruel to <u>me</u> and [–], in taking from <u>us</u> and <u>me</u> our Mother. Oh! My Dear!! sympathize with your dear and bereaved and beloved Newt. I cannot write much— Oh write soon. Your sweet letter of the 21st [–] was rec'd [received] last night. I can't answer it now.

From Your sorrowful
and Dear
Newt

P.S. Don't write for me. [I will] write soon. I will also write and tell you about her funeral etc.

Your Dearest

[ALS, INP, BECHS]

Buffalo Aug. 5th 1862

Sergt. [Isaac Newton] Parker

Dear Sir

Your letter of Aug. 2nd came to hand last evening— I am very glad you informed me the doings of Cusick and Waite, and hope you will keep me posted on their <u>darn</u> speculation operation. When will we Indians cease to be tools for these white devils?— I will explain as far as I am concerned. I was the first man [to] conceived the idea of raising and [an] Indian company and I commenced last November. Shortly afterwards Cusick through Capt. Mitchel got together several Tuscaroras with express purpose of joining Mitchel's Company. These Indians were brought to Buffalo but <u>lo</u> Mr. Fleming would not muster Indians, there they were Cusick thrown out of his position as third or fourth Sergeant for getting these men. When this happened he came right to me, and told me what happened— I told him he better go with all Indians in one company and if he would give him a second lieutenantcy in the company. He said he could furnish 18 to 20 Tuscaroras besides a number of Tonawandas making it all about 30 men. Now I suppose he thinks those men he has are the men he agreed to furnish.

When Col. Shepard came to Buffalo to see if he could get men to intercede for raising a new regiment in this part of the state. A committee was appointed and they gave permits to persons to raise companies— This committee came to me and wanted the Indian Company to join this regiment. I told them we would, and it was agreed to send the men immediately to Elmira.— After the call for 300,000 more men and the state divided into regimental districts the committee informed me that we were to belong to this regimental district and attached to the new Buffalo regiment. This Cusick and Waite (the old man) all agreed to and that was the understanding and it was the express purpose of your being brought from Elmira that you were to go with the Buffalo regiment. But after arriving here Waite had made arrangements with Col. Buckingham and it was a very easy matter for them to get Cusick on their side. A few dollars was sufficient for that <u>Tuscarora rascal</u> to sell our Seneca brothers. Cusick took the advantage while I was away after more recruits,— to go with mustering officers and have the men all mustered in his own name which was in reality in my name— so he <u>stole</u> the men, and was not satisfied with that, goes and <u>sell them for $115.00</u> and a promise of a commission— So you now see who is the blame, am I to blame. He served me a <u>trick</u> which will never be forgotten as long as I live, and for the sake of those men I recruited I will have vengeance. I suppose they think I sold them, but it is no so, Cusick is the man with the assistance of that other sneak Waite, and the man that says I sold them is a liar. Now sir the boys ought not stand this proceedings, and as for your self your sense ought convince you, that you all have all been made the dupe, for satisfying his pockets— Had you all remained here as per agreement we should have had a full company in a short time— He better keep away from Catt. [Cattaraugus] for there are several would like to get hold of him— I will not say what I would do in case he came in contact with me.

Now I will answer those two question in your letter, 1st I am going in with raising a company of Indians, 2nd I will not join Buckinghams regiment for the Indians are consolidated with another company, therefore I cannot go to New York. I wish you could get away some way and assist in getting up this company. I would be willing to take a subordinate position if you could get away and help complete this company— I have notified Col. Buckingham that those Indians are not loitering except the Tuscaroras, and told him if they are not returned, I should apply for their discharge. I also told Mr. Waite that I am— he & I have had quite a spicy correspondence in this swindling game— I told him that you Tonawandas last year were at Geneseo in the Wadsworth guards and were discharged, because you were Indians.

Also another squad from you Reservation was discharged only a short time ago— another company from 50 men of the St. Regis tribe volunteered in the 98th Regt. N.Y.V. have since been discharged, all on account of they being Indians. Now I do not see but you boys can be discharged. again as well as the Indians.— The fact is the general government does not recognize Indians, therefore cannot compel them to do military duty—

Now Brother Newton I want you on the receipt of this, to immediately sit down and answer, and don't you dare to write a shorter letter than this, I want you to tell the boys what I have said, and I want them to give me their ideas on the matter whether I am blamed in this matter, as I have understood that it was all laid to me— They will see by my letter to Sam G. Isaac who is to blame, and also by this. Give me your full opinion on the matter, and I am ever thankful for any information you see fit to send me— answer soon & keep an eye out for the movements of Waite, in fact all the officers—[4]

Very Respectfully Yours,
Capt. C. C. Jemison

[NYSL]

Camp Scroggs—N.Y. City
53rd Regt—
Sunday A.M.
August 17th 1862

My Dearest Wife—

At about 11 o'clock on yesterday forenoon, our Col. came on to the grounds and ordered the whole regiment—upon the parade ground, all that are able to stand. Sick as well. On the occasion, he (the Col.) there informed the Regt that we were under marching orders— To march on the 18th, inst. [instructions] (tomorrow) for Washington and to report ourselves to the Adjutant Genl of the U.S.— The Col has been to Washington for the purpose of getting the Gov bounty for us—of $25 and [a] month's pay in advance of $13 making the sum total of $38. we are promised that amount before we leave the state. I doubt that some [sum]. But says the Col., "If the Gov [Edwin Morgan] orders us on to Washington, with a promise of being paid there, we must like soldiers and like men, without a word of murmur or complaint, but go out only to defend ourselves, but also go to defend the lives of thousands—the Union and the Constitution." Again the Col said, "that if we did not get our money here, he (the Colonel) should try to obtain a 'stay' for the Regt" but I guess we should have to go if we were ordered to— Don't you Dear? I guess so—ain't it— Yes.— For the present, my Dear, you will have to excuse me of my pencil written letters. If you can make them out. Why all right for the object of a communication upon paper is to convey our thoughts and ideas one to another and for the sake of keeping records etc.— Well Dear, I hope that you are well and that you may not be any worse in your illness. Also, furthermore, that you may not have written yet, as requested in my letter one previous to this.— If you have not don't [de]posit [it] until you hear from me again, although oh my "Dear Wife," it's nay much against my heart's desire.— But the fortunes and pursuits of life—and the expanse of the world—may some time vastly separate two dearly and beloved ones. In this, it's a country's call to save a country in danger—and to wipe away Devilism and Rebelism—having God for our shield, our protector, and our spiritual adviser. Aint that so, Wife. I think so. I send the other letter of the 8th just along with this, our dear letter from you.— If you have written, please send for it again and let it go back to you, but send it to our other time. Don't destroy it now, will you Dear. Yes don't for Newt's sake. 3 P.M. Very warm. At 9 A.M. of this day the Col. again came on to the ground[s] and at our herap sack and musket inspection, what is called "Regimental Inspection[,]" he (the Col.) informed us and said: — "It is my good pleasure to inform you that the paymaster was now in town, and that thereby

[Editor's Note: The letter abruptly ends.]

[INP, BECHS]

Camp Scroggs, Red
House Harlem New
York September 1st
1862 Headquarters
53rd Regt N.Y.V.

This certifies that Isaac N. Parker is regularly mustered into the U.S. service (date of muster June 18th 62.) and is attached to Company H. That he has a wife and one child residing in West Seneca St. near Red Jacket Hotel. Buffalo N.Y. And they are in need of relief from your Committee.

1st Sept. '62   Alex Warren Smith
Approved   Capt. Comdg Co. H
Geo. A. Buckingham   53rd Regt N.Y.V.
Colonel Comdg
53rd N.Y.V.

[INP, BECHS]

Camp Life

Monday Evening
7 P.M. 1st Dec., 1862

Beloved Dear[:]

I do think of you so much. You are [in] my continual thoughts and consolation. O Sara, I wish you was here this very minute, how I would choke you and kiss you and, and oh golly what else bite you like sixty.— Well I'll quit and I'll postscript in the morning just on the even of starting.— Samuel G. Isaacs is in Alexandria staying in [the] 85th N.Y. Vols. He will probably come here, only to get his papers of discharge. He will never be fit for service—says he is sick yet in the shoulders.— So tell his friends if any one inquires.— Cusick heard from him. Good night— Dear Happy Dreams of Your Newt.

Tuesday - 2nd

Well My Dear, I am nicely— I had understood[,] for the Major had told me that I was going with the signal Corps— But this morning I went to the Genl Headquarters to report myself for duty. By golly [–] behold the Genl got me to writing, come to find I was detailed to be a copyist in the Generals quarters—golly so, there I was—I said to the Genl for I was thunder struck, says I. I am detailed for the signal Corps. As you'll see I have not as yet left Camp. My name is upon the <u>detail</u> and one other (white) man to be [the] two out of this Regt. I will now tell you briefly how we are going.— two are to be detailed entirely from this Regt and attached to the Signal Corps. To talk on the fields of battle by means of <u>flags</u>. It is not the regular American flag, but it is a flag made expressly for [a] signal flag. In the field of battle; I am to be with the Genl and whatever he commands, I am to transmit his commands to the Cols of the different Regts in the Brigade by means of <u>signal</u> flags. Our Capt has just been here and ordered me to report myself at the Genl quarters at 9:30 on tomorrow morning. So it seems that I am elected sure. Well you'll have to wait until you hear from me again, afore you can write again. O Dear Sara I wish I could hear from you once a week.

Love
Newt

[ALS, INP, BECHS]

Head Quarters, Empire
Brigade, Suffolk, Va.
Dec. 24th 1862
Wednesday Evening, 8 P.M.

Affectionate Dear,

At 4 P.M., we rec'd a <u>dispatch</u> from Division Head Quarters of Suffolk under <u>orders</u> from Head Quarters, Dep't of Virginia 7th Army Corps at and from "Fortress Monroe," to get our entire Brigade in readiness. 3 Brigades are going, of about 16 regiments, 40 rounds in cartridge boxes, and 20 rounds in pockets, 60 in all. I expect to ride a <u>mule</u> along with the Genl and his staff. We are all packed up— Division H.'Qrs. [Headquarters] is now holding telegraph communication with "Fort Monroe." We may start at 12 midnight, maybe in the morning, and maybe not until tomorrow night, under cover of darkness. I wish you a "Merry Christmas." Good night Dear. Don't worry, wait for further news. My love and many kisses to you.[5]

From your Husband Newt

[ALS, INP, BECHS]

Dec. 25th 1862
5 A.M.
Camp Suffolk, Va

<u>My Dear,</u>

I wish you a <u>real</u> "Merry Christmas." Orders prolonged until today. Each soldier is to be equipped all through in clothing ... So we are bent on going sometime today, and on a campaign too, no chance of returning. If shoes are poor, give him a new pair and the full complement of under clothing and 100 rounds of <u>buck</u> and <u>ball</u> to each man 40 with and 60 in company boxes. I am writing in my diary book, holding it in my hand, sitting on my bunk. Went to bed at <u>one</u> and got up at 4:30. Enough for the present. I'll write from the office.

In Haste
Your Newt

Can't write so much today. So it goes, without the full details of news. 8 P.M. It has been a great day. More like the 4th of July than a Christmas Day in the midst of winter.

Your Newt

P.S. I hate to send this until just as we get the command to "Forwards March" or the <u>orders</u> to "fall in." Opinions are that we are bound South towards Chowan River in North Carolina to reinforce a Brigade we have down there under Colonel [Robert Sanford] Foster, Acting Brig. Genl. The <u>orders</u> is to the following effect: "To hold your Brigade in readiness, for the march will be to some distance from this post, and that in all probability it will be a Campaign. — If it is to be a <u>campaign</u> the chances ... we do not return to our (this) camp, but to be moving from post to post, and to hold various positions and to be advancing in our way or another, or else be driven back to our defenses here in Suffolk—our breastworks and forts. — But I know that, that will not be the case, i.e., be driven in. My Dear, I am eager, all on tiptoe, and <u>much</u> in the bargain. Genl has got back from Division H.' Qrs. [Headquarters] Now for <u>news</u> and <u>orders</u>. Look out.[6]

Your Newt

Camp near Newbern, N.C.
Spinola's "Empire Brigade"
Camp—132nd Regt
N.Y.S.V. Infantry
January 15, 1863

My Dear Wife,
    This will be a sort of a journal letter, writing into it occasionally from time to time: For I cannot send it until at such a time arrives. — Our letter communication <u>out</u> from this Dep't is blockaded for the present on account of some <u>expedition</u> preparation and movements in the Dep't. — When all these are completed and started, then I will again open. The story is: an Expedition fitting out, to go by water, for Wilmington, N.C. some 60 [miles] or so, south of here. —consequently Major Genl Foster is cautious in having the <u>fact</u> of this preparation made known, or to reach the "<u>rebels</u>" before the conserted <u>time</u>. — I have written one [–] and the office some a week ago, and I am afraid that it is <u>now</u> lying in the office and maybe <u>this</u> may go with the other at the same time. Well, I need not conjecture on things that I do not know. So with other topics. — At this time we are yet in our camp. No appearance or rumors of our going away as yet. The regt and Brigade that Spencer King is in has gone down further south and west by way of Beaufort. They were here some 3 weeks afore we came. also came from Suffolk. — Well let one see, if I can't or can get my mind collected and thereby get my subjects more properly constructed. Well I'll try to tell you a little about our brigade, regimental and company camps in our Brigade, Regiment and Company Streets, etc. Our brigade camp is about a 1-½ mile[s] a little, southwest of the city, upon a (about) 50 acre field having our exit on the Trent Road—our Reg't and the 158th N.Y.S.V. (1st Reg't in the Brigade) are fronting the Trent Road—158th upon our right. Co[mpany] streets at right angles to the road. — Us <u>2</u> Regts are upon the east line. <u>one</u> upon the south line, <u>2</u> upon the west line and none upon the north line. — The 6th Regt in the Brigade is back of the west line across a little run or swamp [–] way. — We are about half a mile west of the Trent River. The city is almost in sight of our camp. It would be 'if' it were not for a little swamp way. The Brigade is stationed all around this field upon the other edge, reserving the centre for company or squad drills and our Dress Parades. By appearance of the field, it appears that <u>corn</u> was the last crop upon it. The right of our companies nesting on the road on in front of the other— facing north so making our company streets about east and west or some where near it— The co[mpany] cooking places with our regiment is across

the road from us about 50 feet in the rear of this is a little swamp <u>run</u> with the pleasure of washing our faces into it mornings—from 2 to 300 feet in the rear of this <u>run</u> are our company <u>sinks</u>, of course of the military kind. This being, or had been one in the pine woods but now all cut down for wood and huts or part houses.— While in Suffolk in our Reg't, there were some <u>ten</u> women, but now there are only about six or seven, all married and all Irish. Tough aint they?— <u>our</u> is about six months gone for on the increase—all right Direction:

> Sergt. I. N. Parker
> (Co. D 132nd Regt N.Y.V.
> 2nd Brigade.
> 5th Division)
> Newbern, N.C.

I reckon—we have 2 daily drills <u>a day</u> one in the forenoon at 10 and <u>the</u> other at 3 P.M., one of Co. drill and the other of battalion. Col. P. [Peter] G. Claassen resumed command of his Regt on the day before leaving Suffolk.— I'll go back a little upon our march from Suffolk, Va to Chowan River— I have told you that I'd give you some synopsis of it, etc. Dec. 28th 1862 at 9 A.M. the Brigade began to form and fall in for a march. At about 11, we began to move our regimental columns and got under way— Went out on the Edenton road— This was on Sunday. On Sat[urday] afternoon and all Sat[urday] night it rained right smart to Thursday making it very muddy indeed.— The <u>mud</u>, by the time that we came along was about ankle deep, [–] bring the 2nd Regt from the front on right.—and there were six Regts on the road, 4 behind us.—very slippery and water. fine country and level—and swampy. From 11 to eight P.M.: went about 19 or 20 miles— Bivouacked in a grove and rested well and safety. To Monday morning at sun a half an hour high was seen under way.—nothing unusual during the day. went about 18 miles. roads growing better dryer drier— country the same— At 1 P.M. halted some 3 miles before.[7]

Gateville— Messed, <u>coffee</u> and hard <u>tacks</u>, and again under way. march thro Gatesville just as the sun was going down.— Went about 4 miles further, there halted and bivouacked again [at] a Grove—loaded our <u>guns</u> and laid on our <u>arms</u> all night. all [All] arose as usual. Tuesday Morning before sun rise the huge columns were seen arriving. (Says) 13 miles to Chowan River. [The] roads much better. Country [the] same. At 1:30 P.M. halted for rest and to mess —halted 1 and ½ hour, a drizzling rain.— Again forward March. (Says.) 3 miles to the boats. [We] lost our way, and wait 4 miles farther. Got to the Boats at 7:30 P.M. under a rain. Booman's Land-ing. Got on board of our boat at 9 o'clock, and parts of 168th and 171st Pa. Militias. some 1500 in all. Oh awful crowded we are, couldn't go around hardly, down in the hole. Midships—fore and aft casttes and hurricane desk.— Two midships. I had a bunk, "No. 76"—on starboard midship.—at night bodies all over, on the floor, on boxes—barrels, ropes and on piles of knapsacks. Laid to all Tuesday night.— Wednesday A.M. 8 o'clock the fleet got under steam and started. We embarked on the Steamer—"Eastern City"—and General Spinola on the Steamer "Northerner" down Chowan [River] into Albemarle down throo [through] and passed Roanoke Island about 3 P.M., paddling thro[ugh] the night—a little rough— [–] into Pamlico [Sound]—here in sight of New Bern at noon of Thursday January 1st A.D. 1863— We got almost into our dock or place to lay to, when we grounded on a bar taken off by a small steamboat and landed. [We] got here in our camp at sun just doing down. In coming here from Suffolk, lost our way several times, making our trip about 68 miles, and when it could have been made in about 48 miles. No Indians on the entire route, didn't fall out and straggle behind to be picked up by the ambulances. All worried thro[ugh].— Golly I stood it, "like a thousand brick." [We] waded on creek. Ran deep— over my high top boots.— I liked it right well, and could have went all thro[ugh] week just so. As a Regt we done [well] for new troops unused to marching and this was a kind of a forced march, i.e., we had to make the distance in such a time, within a given time— If we came 68 miles, that would be almost 22 miles per day—very good for soldiers, moving so in such a large body. The Army of the Potomac only usually goes from 4 to 8 miles a day. Now we are here, no one knows what we are brot [brought] here for, to fighting of course, I reckon, the when and where is the question. 3 whole Brigades here from Suffolk etc. [–] we were, by orders read at Dress Parade time:—transferred from Spinola's Brigade to that of Brig. Genl. Jourdan's, i.e., our Regt. and the 168th Pa. from Jourdan's Brigade to that of Spinola's—a turn about.[7] Oh what a summer it is here, never did see, have to take a second thought to know that it is in January in the middle of the winter—queer aint it?— Well I must close for this is all the paper I have to my name— My love and many sweet kisses to my sweet Sara.— In dreams I talk with you. In thoughts I see you. Oh if you were here, I would choke you like old forty—would you me?

From Your Husband
I. Newton Parker

[ALS, INP, BECHS]

[Editor's Note: This is a fragment of a letter-journal from Isaac Newton Parker to Sara Jemison Parker, 16 January, 1863]

P.S. 16th 1863—In Camp. My Dear, I made out to find a small piece of paper. As I had your letter finished I last night got your other letter, one of Dec. 11th 1862 and the other of Jan. 3rd 1863— The one of the 11th didn't reach me before we left Suffolk. Dec. 28th rather queer aint it Dear, Oh but wont I [be] glad to hear from you, and to learn that you are in the land of the living and on [–] grounds— I will answer them more fully in my [–] as I have and can put in only just so much into the letter.— But, my Dear I am happy to hear from you, it makes me feel good, and put one in good spirits and fine pleasure on knowing that my dear wife is alive and well. Well there is all kinds of shifting and transferring — Our Regt 132nd N.Y.V. is transferred from Spinola's Brigade to that of Brig Genl J. Jourdan's Brigade.—and another placed in Spinola's Brigade in <u>our</u> place.— So any Dear direct you next thus:— <u>Sergt I. Newton Parker, Co. D. 132nd Regt N.Y.S.V. 2nd Brigade, 5th Division, Newbern, N.C.</u> and I will get it as soon as landed.— Oh 'tis a real summer here. Summer birds are plenty here, and we sweat in our daily drills, as we would in the corn fields in June up north..— Occasionally we have a day and a night or so of rain and wind.— Yesterday and last night it rained and blew a perfect streak— Hoops wouldn't dive down here then. speaking about <u>hoops</u>, that is something our soldiers down here don't see any more. Darn the hoops any way, I don't want to see them at all. Your hoops are <u>mine</u> and that is all I care about. Aint it Dear. Mine is yours and yours are your own—or how is it. What yours are mine and what mine is my own.— Well Dear, six in one and half a dozen in the other—well enough of my nonsense. So I must close. I heard that a boat was going <u>north</u> on Sunday, so I'll mail this on tomorrow down to the city.

Your Dear own <u>Newt</u>

2 P.M. According to the Bulletin at the P. [post] office, the mail will close at 7 this P.M.— I am in town, but most soon go back.— I will write soon as I can again— In Haste,

Your Newt

[ALS, INP, BECHS]

Camp Hitchcock
New Bern, N. C.
Co. "D" 132nd Reg't
New York Infantry,
2nd Brigade, 5th
Division, 18th Corps
de Arme
[undated, early 1863]

My Dear Wife

Your kind favor of the above is duly at hand, and am exceedingly happy to hear from you, for all the scolding you have given me. <u>You</u> now poor son is to blame. I am not to blame for your not receiving my letters. I send them and that is the last I [–] know of it. It must either be in the <u>mail</u> or else in the office at <u>Brant</u>, and I shouldn't wonder but what there was a light "somebody" of the Res[ervation] [Cattaraugus Indian Reservation], who is playing a <u>dead beat</u> upon our letters, making good use of <u>these</u>, <u>his</u> or <u>her</u> long fingers in cabbaging us. I at the same time don't blame you a bit for this note, for of course, you don't know, but my <u>Dear</u> I hope that when this reaches you, you will have them at hand all the letters from here which are of the following dates. 1863 Jan 5th — 17th, 20th and 28th. — and this makes <u>five</u> in all. — Oh my Dear, I hope you may get them. I do wish that you will. Well I'll close off from this and proceed on to another sheet. My Good Dear My <u>Love</u> and sweet kisses to you

From Your Newt

[ALS, INP, BECHS]

Camp Hitchcock
132nd Reg't N.Y.
Infantry. New Bern,
N.C.
Feb. 3rd 1863
Head Quarters Co. "D"
2nd Regt.—2nd Brigade.
5th Division, 18th Army
Corps

My Affectionate Wife,

I will attempt at this cold day to address my dear wife, for it is indeed cold. I got up at six this morning and found it snowing and blowing like old "forty." At 3 A.M. it was a thunder storm, lightning, and rain and wind. It is now 12 n[oon] and its blowing and freezing up right smart. And here I am in my <u>tent</u> without <u>fire</u>, or nothing to warm by during the <u>duties</u> of an "Orderly Sergeant." But it all comes easy. I don't dread it. I am not cold. I am not hungry. And I have got along right well since I have commenced my new duties as an "Orderly." I have had a heap to do, on account of having just moved and again making up new camp and everything "topsy turvey," here and there and nowhere. But I am now getting right well straightened out again so that I am getting the position in shipshape so that I know where I am, and how the Co stands. Cos. [are] all staid in quarters, [with] no drills of any kind. At 2 P.M. [the] regiment fell in for the rations of <u>whiskey</u>. [They] fell in by companies. We have brigade drills on Mondays, Wednesdays and Fridays at 1 P.M. All other weekdays [it is] 9 A.M. Co. drill [is at] 2 P.M. Battalion drill is about the same as I have given you before. I am present quite well ... and I hope that this may find you all well and right side up, alive and kicking—oh my "<u>dear</u>" I hope that you have got all my letters e'er this—for that is all in my mind day and night is thinking of you and the letters and what you must think of your not getting no letters from your far off Newt. But I trust that whatever it may be, maybe all right yet and that the letters when they arrive will explain all for themselves and also this when it reaches you. — How is the weather out your way <u>dear</u>? Any snow yet? or is it muddy as usual, as it was last "Christmas and New Years." I reckon that it must be cold out there, for as a matter of course, it might—to be cold up <u>north</u>. I don't get no newspaper <u>nowadays</u> and got any since our arrival here now 34 days. There are no newspapers sent down here for sale only for subscribers, by officers of the various regiments in this Department.— So you probably know about us, then we do about ourselves, if you notice the proceeding of the Department of North Carolina. — under [the] command of J. G. Foster, Major Genl. I like it more and more every day in this brig.[ade] or that of a soldier's life. — I like to drill, and like to learn something new every day in the way of doing business in the army and of tactics, and of the life <u>out</u> and <u>in</u> camp, in garrison, in the field and on the march on dry ground and in the <u>mud</u> and all over <u>inside</u> and <u>out</u>-side, top and bottom. Golly, I am a soldier, aint I Dear? I hope so, worthy of you, my love, and my Dear, who is my all. My heart is all. It is there all the time. I have [to] get a chance to send [this letter], so I must close. ·Oh my <u>Dear</u> write soon, and tell me everything. Will you? Say yes. My <u>Love</u> and many kisses to you

Your Newt

4th ... Wednesday
P.S. The steamer leaves at 3 p.m. this P.M. for New York City— [– –] try to write. Will you [as] soon as you can.

Your <u>Newt</u>

[ALS, INP, BECHS]

Newbern, N.C.
Thursday
Febry 26th 1863
Six o'clock A.M. In
camp. Camp Hitchcock
132nd Reg't
N.Y. Infantry
2nd Brigade. 5th
Division. 18th Corps
de Armee.

My Dear Affectionate Wife

I learned last night quite late then that a <u>steamer</u> is to leave for the <u>north</u> some time today, so I hasten at this early hours to address you my beloved and dear wife. I am quite well and doing well and I sincerely hope and it is the same good blessing that may be upon your heads by the time that you may receive this. I will give you a brief synopsis of occurrences since the 22nd of this month—"Washington's Birthday." On the 22nd we had to go out to Division Inspection and Review by Genl Prince, and it rained all rained day completely. We let camp at 9 A.M. and back at 3 P.M. wet as rats all [–] and through— That was on the <u>Lord's</u> day too. On yesterday we had a <u>grand review</u> by Major Genl Foster and by the Department. And we had a nice day for it too [was] pleasant over head to under foot too—about 22,000 run out or about 100 acre field—about 2¹/₂ miles from our camp. Genl Foster inspected us first and we passed him in Review and on the whole we had a good time, and I liked it first rate.— Went out at 9 A.M. and back at 2:30 P.M. nice times, lots of spectators. Thursday 21st, 8 P.M., 1863. We [have] been out again today to Genl Foster's Headquarters, a new pole is raised and the "<u>stars</u> and <u>stripes</u>" was let loose to wave in the free breeze of night, at the top of this pole.— While there it began to rain, and it just poured down too, and we were out in our best dress and we got perfectly soaked through. Got back at 12 midnight in the rain. On the 22nd at 5 o'clock p.m. we fell in for our rations of whiskey and this afternoon at 3:30 P.M., we got our rations of whiskey again—an Army gallon— The friends of the boys here are in quite a stew aint they? They have written to Washington to the President asking for discharge of the Indians here. They (the boys here) say that their district attorney and Isaac Halftown and others have come to Washington, says they had council, the councilors did. Do you hear anything about it. I have written a great long letter to the

relations of the boys here through Mr. Asher Wright. You may hear of it—
by sister[–in–law] Martha. My (Dear write often you will won't you, oh yes
—do Dear.[8]

From Your Dear Husband
I. N. Parker

[ALS, INP, BECHS]

Camp Hitchcock
132nd Reg't N.Y.
Infantry, 5th Division.
18th Army Corps.
Newbern, N. C.
April 3, 1863
Co "D" In Camp

My Dear Wife[,]

I will endeavor to be improving all the little opportunities which may be present themselves; in trying to pen a few lines again to you.—although, this may reach you at the same time that my last one will.—which I forwarded only a few days ago.— In the absence of any yet from you, I will keep a writing at such times as time affords me.— I ever trust, that in the kind Providence of <u>God</u>, all of my communications may ever reach you well, and find you in health.— I will only relate my points in briefs; room not allowing it in detail— On the 1st last, their was all day long heavy cannonading to the northward of us, report says. That it is at a place called Little Washington about 30 miles to the north of us, by Genl Spinola and his brigade:— I know that Genl Spinola has gone out in that direction some six days ago.— Again on the 3rd last the cannonading in the same direction is plainly heard and on that day rumors became quite rife, that we are to march out there to reinforce Spinola, which seems quite probable in my mind and in which I wish we would go.— I only wish that we aint gone afore now,—disappointed quite so. Here is also a rumor, and seem quite authentic to me. It came in a few evenings ago to the effect that the President of the United States refuses to pay the 132nd Reg't on account of its being so mixed up with the old 53rd Reg't N.Y.V.— The President demands that he (the Pres[ident]) wants to now how many of there are of the old 53rd rank, file and [the] like, who are consolidated with this 132nd, and how many there are of the original 132nd from the officers down to a private. When this is ascertained then the President will cause the 132nd to be paid so the matter stands. We are partly under marching orders. Our Capt. has ordered 2 days rations to be cooked—and that says we may go either tonight or tomorrow morning at 4 o'clock or so. I suppose you read of us occasionally in the war news of the day. [–] I have been ailing for the past 2 days but am getting better.— Hoping these few lines will reach you well as it quite "Lovable in health."— I write in much haste.— My Love and many kisses to my Dearest. Oh Sara how much I do dream of you, good dreams too. — I always feel good and glad for some time after. — Now dear write soon and tell me how much of a spring you are having out there up north.

From Your Dear Husband
I. N. Parker

[ALS, INP, BECHS]

Co. D
132nd Reg't N.Y.
Inftry. 2nd Brigade.
5th Div. 18th Army
Corps. Newbern, N. C.
May 17, 1863
In camp. Sunday evening

My Dearest Wife:

I will endeavor to avail myself of the present opportunity to send another of my heartfelt thanks, full of appreciation and worth to whom I know [now] address. One of the Gov[ernment] steamers arrived in port on yesterday afternoon about 5 or so and leaves again on tomorrow evening. She brought our northern mail but am sorry to say that there was nothing for poor me. Oh! Dear! I wish I had got one from you. Don't care about [one] from my house [at the Tonawanda Indian Reservation]. One from you would have <u>really</u> done me so much good—ah aint it so Dear? Well I'll commence on business now.— By the <u>Providence</u> of <u>God</u> with life and health, it is my purpose if permitted by my commanding <u>officers</u> to visit you on a "furlough" long about and during the month of September. If all of the above will be my fortune, I will try to leave here (providing we are here in Newbern) by the first steamer on and from the <u>first</u> of September which in all probability may leave during the first week of September and which by the guidance of the <u>Spirit</u> of the spirits, i.e., "The <u>Great Spirit</u>" will bring up into Buffalo some time about the 12th to the 15th of September. I tell you this much of my mind and prayers, my good Dear but soon don't at present make too much calculation upon it. Only let us hope and pray that we both may be made happy on meeting again for which to <u>God</u> in heartfelt thanks we must be. Oh yes, to see each other again. Take each other in each one's arms with that fond embrace which we were always want to do.— It will be my heart's desire, and in which I will do: to have most of my visit with you. My trip at home [Tonawanda Indian Reservation] will be short and my stay elsewhere will also be short, but the most of the time that I may have will for you, for you and I to enjoy together.— You will find this at your office I trust long about the last of this month which will make it three months from then. Long about the first of next month I want to send somethings to you for Ex: some for repairs etc. The steamer (I learn) [–] leaves on tomorrow afternoon or ev[ening]. Now good girl, my dear girl! Write soon and often? —Will you? Yes—that's a good Dear. Love and misses to my Dear Wife.

From your Dear Husband
Newt

[ALS, INP, BECHS]

I. Newton Parker
132nd Reg't N.Y.S.
Vols. Out Post Camp
Hoffman Co[mpany]
H.' Qr's. [Headquarters]
Newbern
Department of North
Carolina June 21st 1863.

Explanation,

You will observe that by taking hold at No. 1 between thumb and fore-finger, face upwards and turning No. 1 over from your body, you <u>wind</u> the watch in keeping the watch in the same manner but pressing No. 2 down with your left thumbnail and keeping hold of No. 1 as before you can set the time by turning No. 1 either way:—either over from you or over to-wards your person.— Take the <u>watch</u> to O. E. Sibley (if the name is right)[.] I think [he is] across from and a little above Seneca St[reet] on <u>Main</u> [Street].—and let him read this. The watch has not been cleaned in <u>seven</u> years and there is something the matter of the inner <u>point of No. 2</u>. I want it <u>cleaned</u> and <u>repaired</u> thoroughly, for I send it north for that express pur-pose. To have it cleaned up aright—and I have that business confidence in Mr. Sibley that I have taken pains to have my work don up in a workman-ship like manner.— When the job is finished, you take the watch, after a due trial in running by hanging <u>still</u> in the shop for a few weeks: and give it a trial to see how it will run by carrying. It will run [a] full 48 hours before it will run down. made and brought over from Germany on last May a year ago.— I know myself that it is a splendid time keeper when it is all right.— for I knew it to be so before it was; by strange hands, quite injured.— It was injured as it is thought at the point No. 2. That No. 2 was not pressed down enough at the time that an effort was made to move the hands in setting the time, or as the watch venders here think, that it was something to that effect. But I will not trust it in none of their hands down here for they are nothing but the unfinished apprentices of our northern cities and some not even knowing the difference between a "balance wheel" and "main spring"—for such are a large class of the civilian money suckers who are tagging after the federal army in this land of "Dixie."— Report to me Mr. Sibley's opinion of the supposed dirty and injured watch—and of the probable success.[9]

Out Post
Camp Hoffman. 132nd Reg't N.Y.
Infantry
Bachelor's [Batchelder's] Creek, N.C.
August 15th 1863
near Newbern
Company "D" in Camp.

Sister[–in–law] Martha [Hoyt Parker]
  If it will be some what interesting to you and the folks, I will give you a faint synopsis of our present military duties. We are the exterior out post from and the key to Newbern which in a military phrase is called a <u>post-of-honor</u>, that is, a post of the highest trust entrusted to a body of soldiers in active campaign. After Burnside captured this place, i.e. Newbern, the post was occupied by the 27th Mass. Vols. Relieved by the 58th Pa. Vols. and upon the death of thier [their] (the 58th) noble Col. men were selected by General [J. G.] Foster, upon the high recommendation of the high military officials in Newbern given of us to take the 58th which we accordingly did on the 25th of last May. We commenced our (apparent) good name in N.Y. The N.Y. press praised us as in fact of being the best regiment of General Spinola's Brigade and second to none of the N.Y. City regiments that had then left for the seat of War. Although the body of the regiment were at the time ignorant of our good name, we improved upon our good name during our stay in Suffolk from Sept. 28th '62 to Dec. 26 '62. We staid [stayed] in Newbern as a garrison force until we came home. During our stay in Newbern we kept ascending our ladder of fame slow, but apparant sure. We hold a front here of nigh seven miles running at right angles to the R.R. [railroad] and the R.R. [railroad] being the center of our line. Then there are six miles more, 3 miles upon each flank, that are picketed by cavalry. But in the two recent expeditions from here, the cavalry were drawn off and then we picketed those six miles, making nigh 13 miles of front and me, not having now, 600 effective men. We are considered bold in holding so large a front— and lively will be the time whenever we will be attacked, but that is rather doubtful, for it is difficult of access to our camp or fort, being much surrounded by swamps and heavy pine wood lands for miles around, so much so that heavy artillery can't come in, and hard for infantry to penetrate in so on the whole we are right well fortified by the country itself. Our camp is on the south bank of Bachelor's [Batchelder's] Creek emptying in the Neuse and on the side of the track. We are blessed with all the conveniences we can ask. We have a

signal station attended by a signal corps working both by flags and signal telegraph line from Beaufort to here and then we have two branches from here one off to the left to a post called Red House near or on Trent road and running from there to Deep Gully[,] a few miles further on. And another off to the right running over to the Washington Road near Strut's ferry on the Neuse. These two branches are to be operated both by signal flags and telegraph and we are accommodated by ears to Newbern and Beaufort by which all our provision and clothing and all are transported up to us. Our rides all free, a soldier going north has a free passage to N.Y. City, what more can a soldier ask of a government for which he is serving in. A signal watch tower is built right over the track at our depot to 8 feet high looking up and down the track and up and down these two branches which I spoke of. In these two branches the trees are felled about a road wide giving a full scope for the glasses. We have two telegraph lines up to here. A signal field telegraph, a process of laying the telegraph as an army advances in the field of battle and an army telegraph for sundry purposes pertaining to the service. In our camp upon our color line we have a play staff some 90 feet high of a single stick—called "a <u>post</u> flag staff". Then we have presented to us <u>post-colors</u> of the first quality, some 50 ft. by 20. It is large splendid flag—presented to us by Genl Foster. I take Genl Foster to be right smart and of the right stamp. He is a sharp hawk eyed looking man, heavy mustache on his eye brows, weight about 200 or over, abouthalf gray in hair rather inclined for a large corporation. I have full confidence that he'll prove himself worthy of the additional Dept. attoled to him and of his wider scope of operation and Dix is in the right place of the right troop. But lo, although over 1300 miles from home, get me not out of the reach of <u>death</u>. Death reigns amongst us. He sways his scepter of death in our ranks, regardless of positions. We are victims of the various diseases peculiar to the southern clime among the hot beds of cotton, and in the forest of pines each clothed and glistening with pitch, streaming down their grand trunks like water [–] by the heat, almost ready to take fire. But we must each abide by our respective lots and only cast our hopes and faith and our prayers upon the protector of [–] to protect and guide us through the various trials to which we may be subjected. But I must close, having already devoted too much space and intruded too much upon your precious and motherly time. I had got thus far with this lengthy detail when to my joy came your very unexpected, but sisterly letter, bringing to me such consolation a serves a meal to my hungry heart—and to my longing spirit of thirst for some thing good and lovely, of words of encouragement to a soldier who is battling the storm and front of a rebellion such as any

<u>enlightened</u> nation never saw.— At some other time I'll answer your kind letter and endeavor to dwell upon other topics, which I trust will serve as a reading past-time for you when all <u>our</u> little pappooses are asleep in their quid—and angelic dreams, oh happy are they for they know no care; peace be with them and may their gray hairs be blessed. Tell Frankie, Fredie and Minnie that uncle Newt (the candy uncle) remembers them well. I don't know <u>prince</u> Albert nor William <u>Tell</u>. Well my long pen must <u>halt</u>. Remember me to all kind well-wishing friends— My grandmother (I forgot which anyhow) Jennie Shearer. Mr. and Mrs. Wright [Asher and Laura Wright], that's all I know—we got a "Monitor" ironclad box car placed on car wheels, and mounting two rifled steel parrot-guns [Parrott gun] at each end— each gun having 3 different ranges —front, rear, and upon each flank— Genl Peck of Syracuse is our new commander in this department under Genl Foster. Pick was in Suffolk Va. when we were there— a Major Genl also—you need not write until I write again. I am "right smart" in health and hope this may reach you the same.[10]

> From Your Brother-in-Law
> and Soldier
> Newt

[ESP, APS]

Out Post near Newbern
N. C.
Monday Evening
8 o'clock Oct. 5th,
1863

Affectionate Wife,

My Dear, Your kind and loving letter has come by train and am happy indeed to hear from you. Oh my! I am in a great hurry and therefore am writing in haste. A week ago today since we commenced to work in building our winter quarters by raising small logs 3 feet high then past our tent on top of that, clot the chinks with clay and build chimneys. I am [–] and building chimney to [–] now. I got a letter from Carrie [Caroline Parker] of the 20th last in which I learn of the sickness of my Father [William Parker] confined to his bed and the doctors gave him up—says won't get well. Oh he may be <u>no more</u> this hour.— I am looking forward for the next boat to bring me the sad news —Well <u>God</u> knows whats for the best.— When I get straightened up in my new quarters, I will then write more. [I am] afraid that you can't now read this. I have written it in such a hasty way. Dear me I aint got no more time now. Hoping you are well as I am about that.— My Love and many kisses to my Dear wife.

From your Dear Husband
I. N. Parker

Enclosed I send you some change for candy for I know you like sweet things too—don't you Dear. I know you do—don't we? Yes thats a good Dear. Tell me will you, yes do.

I.N.P.

P.M. Tuesday 6 A.M. —

Last night the officers of our regiment got up from Newbern [N]egro singers or minstrels of 3 violins—1 banjo—1 tambourine and bass violin.— They played, danced and sung in front of the Col and Lt. Col's quarters. They had a gay old time of it— I tell you. In the Evenings I am fixing up a little in the inside by littles [letters?] and that is what keeps me busy. Right sharp this morning—air cool and sharp. I believe it makes you feel better in these sharp morning[s]. How is the weather out your way. Dear— the [–] etc.

Your Newt

[ALS, INP, BECHS]

Co. "D" 132nd Reg't. N.Y.
Infantry Bachelor's [Batchelder's] Creek
near: Newbern, N.C.
Out Post. Camp Hoffman
Sunday Evening, Oct. 18th
1863

My Beloved Wife

In the absence yet of any letter from you, I write again, hoping this may find you in good health and enjoying yourself totally, or well enough considering times and circumstances etc and of your dear husband being off to War.—all fact[s] together I presume go to make up a feeling and a desire of a kind and dearly concernment for all things and for <u>him</u> in particular, i.e. me, your Newt. [Lieutenant Cornelius C.] Cusick returned on last Friday afternoon, in great style, with a new suit of military clothes throughout, and part of his equipments are new also. I learnt that he has been to Catt. [Cattaraugus]. I have not talked with him as yet. had no time, for he had been in picket, came in on yesterday. Cusick got a letter from Doc Wilson [Dr. Peter Wilson] and I read it. It says about Hatt Pierce,—aint time or [–]—now to tell you, and maybe you don't care about my telling you etc.— We have rumors in camp that we are going to reinforce Genl [Q. A.] Gilmour at Charleston. I am inclined to credit the story. says [Says] to be [–] in [–] of next month.—if it turns out true, I'll be glad. Another is that we are to have a new Genl in Newbern in place of [General John James] Peck, a one Genl Harney or Arney, or some such name, an officer of the <u>regular</u> Army and been through the "Mexican War." I guess this is true too—but you may see it in the press before it reaches us etc— I have not felt well in [–] now for some time, having my quarters now finished, I'll have more time to write, and which I am [–] to do—for in case we are moved from here I <u>must then</u> do it, and that right now. I have a hand[written] <u>Will</u> in course of completion for my Wife Sarah—my beloved and Dear Partner in life!— Our Co. "D" on last evening just after retreat appeared before our Capt. quarters and presented to him a gold watch with a silk Guard clasped with a gold slide in all worth about $140.00 or so.—gotten up by the company by subscription. I gave $2.00 towards the enterprise. Two 3 rousing cheers were then given. Cusick acted as spokesman. I'll sign no more subscription papers. "I can't see it."—that's played out with me.— A boat is expected today or tonight—the steamer "Albany." Is the why of my writing this in advance, so as to have it in time. I am anxious to learn about the progress of the watch for I need one all the time, my not having one may at times get [me] into trouble while on certain kind of duty: picket or some thing else. — I got a letter from sister Carrie [Caroline Parker] in which she tells me that Ed Green has enlisted again in Buffalo — Great Fool! for money [military bounty] I reckon. The way she wrote, I guessed that she has kindly fell out with Cusick. — Oh! says my old Father is yet alive, but now very low. Well, there is no dashing a way of, "the cap of affliction" for it is as <u>God</u> sees fit for his fellow creatures. My Dear write soon. My Love and many kisses to you my sweet Dear— I dream of you often, good pleasant dreams too— Don't you dear?— Enclosed I send to you for some thing to keep you even sweet [– –], aint it Dear. Good night.[11]

From Your Dear Husband
I. N. Parker

[ALS, INP, BECHS]

Co. "D" 132 Reg't
New York Infantry
Bachelor's Creek
near Newbern,
N.C. Out Post.
Camp Hoffman
Wednesday, Nov. 4th,
1863

My Dear Wife,

I am deprived the knowledge of your where-abouts, and therefore am now restrained from writing much or saying much and it is not <u>policy</u> were it in your case and as it is <u>now</u> mine to write much more until hearing from, or of your where-abouts. But I trust and hope that nothing of a serious character has befallen you—or that no move has affronted you.— The last heard from you is now full and over a month ago. I can't write on business until hearing from you— I am well and hope the same of you. My ever Love and many kisses to my wife.—

From Your Husband
I. N. Parker

[ALS, INP, BECHS]

Co. "D" 132nd New York
Infantry Bachelor's [Batchelder's]
Creek near Newbern
N. C.
Outpost. Camp Hoffman
Sunday Evening,
Dec. 27, 1863

My Dear Wife,

I write to my dear wife from love and an unceasing remembrance of our mutual endearments and affections and of our devotedness to each other. It is my trust and prayer in <u>God</u> that this may reach my wife well and enjoying times totally and comfortably according to our being so far separated in space but yet oh my Dear, our affections, our ever flowing love and dear remembrances of our endearments are not broken or separated by space or time but on the reverse. Time makes it wax older and firmer, purer and nobler, the space makes it strong. It is strong in chain. It glitters by constant rise, and it is elastic that eventually it will again draw us together and spring us again into each others fond embrace. Then oh my Dear, we ought to be thankful to our <u>God</u> and protector in permitting us to meet again. Aint it my Dear. Oh how I hope that you are well and that again your eyes will be entirely well, if not nearly so.

On the 20th last, our captain appointed and detailed me as "Sergeant Color Bearer" to carry the <u>United States Colors</u>, and another besides me, who carries

[Editor's Note: The letter ends abruptly.]

[INP, BECHS]

Rochester, New York
Dec. 14, 1863

Maj. Genl. Benjamin Butler
Fortress Monroe, Virginia

Dear Sir:

I desire to commend to your favorable notice a young Seneca Indian, a native of this State, now serving as a non-commissioned officer in Co. D., 132 Reg. N.Y. V. and stationed at Newbern, North Carolina.

He has been in the service for a year and six months, and his friends would be much gratified if he would now be commissioned as a Captain. He is qualified, I am told, to sustain an examination for a Captain position.

Sergeant Isaac Newton Parker, for is his rather formidable English name, is the son of a Seneca Chief who now draws a pension for services as a soldier in the War of 1812. His brother Ely S. Parker, formerly an engineer in the civil service of this state and of the U.S. is now a captain in Genl. Grant's army. He is also a Seneca Chief of higher rank than his father. This family is the most talented Indian family of the Iroquois stock and is of the Red Jacket blood.

Apart from these antecedents which are of but little account among us— I think you would find young Parker worthy of your favor and encouragement upon his own merits. The reports which his friends secure from him are favorable.

This is enough to place him once in your mind: and if you think of him a second time something will result from it to his advantage.

Yours respectfully
L[ewis] H[enry] Morgan

[ALS, Isaac Newton Parker Compiled Military Service Record, Office of the Adjutant General, RG94, NA]

Combat

Co. "D" 132nd New
York Infantry
Bachelors Creek
near Newbern,
N. C.
Camp Hoffman, Jan. 3,
1864

My Dear Wife

In my last letter I told you of a <u>secret</u>. Well we went out on that but didn't see a nary <u>reb</u>—went to "Trenton" on <u>Trent River</u> some 18 miles from here. It rained all the time too. Now today at 3 P.M., we start again on another scout, only <u>one</u> company from this Reg't and the rest in [the] cavalry, the 12th New York—we this time are to go mounted too going out on "Core Creek" some 18 or 20 miles from here to take a Guerrilla camp by <u>surprise</u> on and long about daylight on tomorrow (Monday.) We have got to steal our way there and then make a <u>charge</u> on the <u>camp</u> as our only chance of success—<u>dash</u> into them to the top speed of one "crow-bates" [?]. I hope you are well, or quite so. I am right smart indeed in health etc. A boat is in at Beaufort below here, and the <u>mail carrier</u> has just started for our mail but he won't be back again [before] we start. My Love and many kisses to my sweet <u>Dear</u>

In Haste
Your Dear
Newt

[ALS, INP, BECHS]

Map of Union Forces at New Bern, Notes of Battle of Batchelor's Creek, Feb. 1, 1864 and other notes, May 10, 1864, Sergeant Isaac Newton Parker, "Color Bearer" 132nd N.Y.V. Infantry

Taken from a <u>*Bird's Eye*</u> *view of the* <u>*Mind's Eye*</u> *By - I. Newton Parker, Serg't Co "D" & "Color Bearer" 132nd N.Y.V. Infantry*

On February 1st 1864— Fight—the most fighting was at the "Neuse Road Bridge" from 2:30 till 9:30 A.M. They drove us down the road and R.R. like hot cakes. Our train ran their battery at the R.R. Crossing." The Enemy came down the "Neuse" and Trent <u>roads</u>.— On the 3rd the little garrison at "Beach Grove" surrendered. [William] Kennedy boy with them. Along <u>all</u> the <u>rivers</u> and <u>creeks</u>[,] it is very <u>swampy</u> and all the <u>open</u> places on the map is <u>pitch pine timber</u> interspersed with <u>swamps</u> come large and small—so that it is impossible for troops.

I.N.P.

The 132nd furnishes the men from "Neuse Road Bridge" to "Burnt Church" and "Tuscarora [North Carolina]." Distance of <u>our</u> "line" about 5 and 1 to "Tuscarora[,]" in all about "<u>six</u> miles"—

Two companies (at present) of the 158th N.Y.V are at "Beach Grove"—and <u>Three</u> at the "Red House"— We [–] with them at "Burnt Church"—

The 12th N.Y. Cavalry and some infantry commands the "Trent Road[,]" Colonel Savage[,] Comdg Post.

Colonel Claassen commands the <u>Creek</u> and "Red House included and "Beach Grove" also.

Long the [– – –] the 132nd has seen the time when [–] done the entire picketing from "Beach Grove" to "Deep Gully"— [– –] "Neuse" road bridge—"R.R. Block House"— Burnt Church— Red House and [–]—a distance by the picket <u>line</u> of some 13 miles, more or less. When Burnside captured New Berne, his troops had some hard fights at "Red House" and "Burnt Church"— The rebels burnt the church and thus the <u>spot</u> is named. It was a "Baptist [–] Communion Church." "Red House" is called after the <u>red house</u> that stands on the spot over 70 years old—all riddled by shots— "Pine Tree"—after a solitary <u>tree</u> standing in the <u>centre</u> of a large plantation— "Deep Gully," a swamp stream—some thing and very much like when Widow Love [–] went to live at the one [Tonawanda] State School House— "Tuscarora" use to be a R.R. Depot—but the buildings at the <u>depot</u>—mills and [–] are all long ago burnt.

May 10th A.D. 1864—
The 132nd will have the honor occupying these Out <u>Posts</u>[,] the <u>key</u> and back <u>bone</u> [backbone] of <u>New Berne</u>: will be a year on the <u>25th</u> day of this month. Perhaps such <u>honor</u> of doing <u>outpost</u> duty has not been <u>conferred</u> upon any other regiment in this present "Rebellion."

[In] Memory to the 132nd Reg't N.Y.V. Infantry

[ALS, ESP, APS]

Co. "D" 132nd Reg't N.Y.V. Infantry.
Bachelor's Creek
near New Berne, N.C.
Out Posts. In Camp.
April 1st A.D. 1864

Dear Sister[–in–law] Martha [Hoyt Parker]

Don't be afraid. I won't send you no "April fool" letters. No I won't. I will write you one in a right down good earnest. So you need to have no occasion to "laugh and grow fat"— So sit you down now with specs on and peruse these few scribled lines from one who is "far away"—from one who is "afar off over hills and plains and the deep blue waters."— Friday has came in for the first of April, which is an unlucky day, according to the old saying of our old "sires," but we foolish young things do not care about noticing such freaks in our old people.

"April showers bring May flowers"

That I believe applies to the north, for down here the: "January showers brought forth February flowers."— This day looks very loweringly indeed— Well I hardly know what to write, only that I want to be adoing some thing, for I have nothing to read or anything else, wherein I can occupy myself in some way half way decent — We have a "theatre" and a "bowling alley," but I don't indulge in the follies of either or patronage either, for to sustain them—

7 P.M. I have been gone about all day. went away at 9:30 A.M. and got back to camp at 3:30 P.M. been round through the country (of course) inside of our lines— At 4 this p.m. we sent down to New Berne two full blooded spies. We caught them inside of our lines on yesterday morning. There are six of them in all— Four are yet at large— They were seen north west of our camp about two miles from here early this morning, trying to work their way through the lines—they may try it—most mighty hard tonight and it is raining to and has been since 5 o'clock and they may try it in the dark hours of night— It is now bunking time and I must quit. It is raining hard.

[April] 2nd. Rained hard all night and all day till 3 P.M. when it thought best to take pity on us by quiting and instead of rain it is now going to be "a right smart cold night"— I have found out to my dreaded satisfaction what will become of me, if I ever fall into the hands of the enemy—either with a whole skin or in a wounded state. neither will help me. If I am captured "whole," the first thing will be they (the captors) will demand and if I don't accede, they will take every thing of any value, in money and articles, off from my person and then they will conduct me to the "rear" of their forces— If the Enemy should find me on the field in a wounded state, unable to help myself they will riffle me of every thing about me, and either leave me to die, or take me to the "rear," or, and which is the worst of all, either dispatch me to the "unknown regions"—to which place, I might not be in none to much hurry to go to— Or, and which is the last of all, if I am shot dead upon the field, and the Enemy gets to me, they will take <u>every thing</u> down to my very <u>shirt</u>. (Now I'll tell you my authority for my assertion— In one late (Feb. 1st) fight, what men of ours were killed and left behind I will relate a case or two— 1st Lieut. Arnold Zenette, Act'g Qtr. Mts [Acting Quartermaster] [was] killed. The Rebs buried him after stripping the body to its very cotton knit-<u>shirt</u>. He had on a splendid suit of clothes [and] fine silver watch, high boots, $7.00 woolen shirt.—and <u>all</u> your [–] except the shirt, and buried with <u>toes</u> and <u>hands sticking</u> out of the ground, and all <u>crampt</u> up at that—a soldier killed in a large open field buried where he fell in a perfect made state. One soldier out of our Co. [company] shot right through the temple and fell dead at the "breastworks" and left behind was also in the same condition—a soldier (private) in the 17th Mass. V. [Volunteers] had both his legs and the knees, shot-off by a cannon's solid shot. His comrades picked him to carry him back, but he beged [begged] [them] to let [him] alone, saying that he knew that he could not live. He was burried where he fell, also being robbed of its [his] clothing. Several of our men were captured who again had the good luck to get away. they were <u>all</u> without exception had been robbed of <u>all</u> of their affects [effects], in "green backs," watches, coats, boots, caps, etc.— The man who was killed by a solid shot near Newberne, (the one I saw) his shoes and stocken [stockings] were taken the rest being unfit—being torn by the shot. The ball passed on his left side midway between the "hip" and "arm," but it took off the "left arm" at the shoulder and tore to atoms over half of the body. poor fellow didn't know what killed him.

But I must close as perhaps letters of this kind are not over interesting—and also that I am not an apt person to write an interesting one, and hardly a sensable one—but of that lay it to <u>no one</u> except my own poor self. Oh! Think not of my once, good old Mother, who I am confident now reigns in heaven among the crowned ones—nor of my good old sire, who is now as it were, with <u>one foot</u> in the "grave"— Ah say not one word "ought" of them, but to <u>me</u> and me <u>alone</u>. But enough. I am always writing on thins that you care nothing about, and things that don't concern you, or any body else, but says: "we are all <u>dependent</u> creatures"—one upon another, and the whole with one great <u>Creator</u>—<u>God</u>.— Remember me to all in kind remembrance.

Ever Your Brother
I. Newton Parker

[ALS, ESP, APS]

Co. "D" 132nd N.Y.V. Infantry
Infantry. Bachelor's
Creek near New Berne,
N. C.
"Camp Claassen"
May 7, 1864

My Dear Wife—

    I write you again to learn if possible of the break off of your part of our once correspondence. I want to ascertain from you <u>yourself</u> before I say a word one way or the other and if I can't that way, I will then wait until I came north as I have a promise from my Col <u>in writing</u> to that effect. How soon I will not say. I have not had a letter from you now in <u>three or four months</u> and you may think the error lies with me. If so, say it and let me know. I for my life can't ascertain <u>what the matter can be</u>. Must a rupture occur between <u>you</u> and <u>me</u>?— Oh! <u>God</u> forbid!!— I will say nothing nor conceive nothing. Nor make a mountain out of a "mole hill" until I <u>can her from you</u> or see you in person—<u>face-to-face</u>.— If this reaches you, I invite a hearing from you.

Ever Truly Your Dear Husband
I. Newton Parker

P.S. You may have e'er now heard of my late affliction of the death of my only surviving Parent—a Father— Home is <u>no home</u> for me, without my Father and Mother— Now, now my <u>only</u> sister is the only family tie that will ever call me— If in the mercy of <u>God</u> my <u>life</u> may be spared for a few years more— Oh! let us console each other—for so knowing how soon it may be <u>your turn</u> to lose a Mother and Father— I can't write much.

INP

[ALS, INP, BECHS]

Camp Claassen 132nd N.Y.V. Inftry
June 26th 1864
Sunday Even'g (Hot indeed)

My Dear Sister [Caroline Parker]

It is so awful and mighty hot for the last few days that it seems almost
impossible for man or beast to move about in the sun—laying in my tent as
quiet as possible, and then the sweat will ooze out and pour down my
weather beaten physique just as though I was under a dripping tub— I will
commence with what is foremost in my mind.— I have thought of it long
afore now, but then at that time, you had much, to do. It is— If you have yet
the moccasin[s], I wish you would send it without delay, and soon as convenient. I need them very much indeed through the middle of the hot days of
our warm weather. Our heavy government shoes are unbearable in the
hotest part of a hot day. Together with, if possible two pudding sticks and
two ladels [ladles]—the pudding sticks to be of different sizes and makes,
as well as the ladles. With the mocassin[s] please send two or three pairs of
light summer socks. I have formed acquaintances and became quite inti-
mate of friendly terms with two good families—here at Bachelor's Creek.
One of the family has a daughter, a tailoress by trade[,] and she has done a
considerable of little job work of one time and another, all of which she has
done for me gratuitously, and had she made charges would [− − − − −] not
more [− − −] when I were perfectly tired of government rations, I would
strole out either of the houses and would invariably partake of a good hearty
meal and it would be four times out of six that I wouldn't be charged anything at all—and generally all among the citizens of this creek, the price
per meal is 30 cents—per table plate size—25—biscuits per dozen, 3- cts—
eggs 40 & 50 cts—onions per dozen 20 cts—and now I desire to recipro-
cate, although in a small way; their very home—like kindness to me per-
sonally, and also too, more particularly of these two families and now if you
please to be kind enough, to be to the trouble, and, if possible, within the
bounds of means to get the articles with to do so and forward them to me
[− −], and I shall trust and hope that I may receive them during the coming
month—I have had the misfortune to lose one of those handkerchiefs you
sent me—and I have only one of the white handkerchiefs, I brought from
home. I have thought of this, some time ago, but then I knew that it could
not be conveniently done. You have some idea of the kind and quality of
government rations, —if you do, you must then expect soldiers to get mighty
tired of it, now & then; and it is then a most pleasant treat, and very refreshing to the soldier's weary nature, to partake at such times a real home

raised and home cooked vituals, although of no great variety, nor of the richest of kind—but oh it is [– – – – –] southern garden greens—sweet [–] potatoes—several kinds of lettuces—peas—onions—cucumbers—beets—etc— of meat—kind mostly beacon [bacon]—of bread kind—comdodgers— dumplings—apple or berry, baked or boiled,— wheatflour—short cake— and light-bread—and biscuits. Another reason, why I would like the things, is, because, I do no duty, i.e., in going out on picket, or in camp on guard duty—all I have to do is, to attend the <u>colors</u>—and consequently I am in camp a large portion of the time lying in my tent wallowing over in my perspiration except—only at such times as when I am out in the country, as we call it. But if after all [is] said and done, the things are not to be had, or the where - withs to get them with; why thus I can't help it and can say nothing more—cause us poor devils aint got no money, and no prospects when we will only that it is, "get pay tomorrow"—"get pay next week" and all such stories, but devil a pay do we get. Things and matters have been quieter[,] quiet since our return from Kinston—although rebel scouts are hovering along our lines, fishing to pick off our picket posts—i.e. capture and take them off and [– –] will try I hope, to let them know your mind whenever convenient, about the things of which I ask. I of course can't urge it, if it comes hard or grudgingly, for I am well-aware that I have the power to make preemptory demands on our family resources, being as you have intimated to me of limited character— But it so awful hot I must close

Your [–] Brother
Newt

I have put on to this letter the last stamp I had to my name—and nary [–] have I, to get any more with—and therefore I'll have to lay off, to sweat and blow over Uncle Sam's snail like movements with his "greenbacks" until he does come—and will only have to quiet my self down to—a poor soldier's lot.—who has enlisted for <u>3</u> years or sooner shot.

N[ewt]

[ALS, ESP, APS]

Goldsboro, N.C., April 1st
1865 Camp 132nd N.Y.
V. Infantry 1st Brigade,
1st Division, Army of
Beaufort

Mr. Wright

Reverend Sir:—

It becomes my painful duty and I am obliged to ask you in return, in addition with some trouble that you would be to: To please inform Mrs. Widow John Hudson, that her son Foster is now no more. He died from the effects of his wound in the General Hospital at New Berne on the 23rd ultimo, at 2 o'clock in the afternoon. Please do send for her and reveal the sad news to her in person—painful yet it must be told and the intelligence must be given [–] a little recapitulation, and I believe (if I remember correctly) that I have written to you about the sad event of his wound and to reveal the same to his widowed mother with words of encouragement, consideration and a dear hope. Recapitulation: He was wounded about 3 o'clock of the afternoon of the 7th of March. Reached Newbern on Thursday the 9th and on Friday the 10th his leg was amputated. The wound was upon the left knee joint. The ball entered the socket base or head of the shin bone and not exactly in the socket joint. The ball did not go entirely through. It lodged in about halfway. The amputation was made about half way up the thigh or upper leg and strong hopes were entertained [for] his recovery until the day of his death. He died of hemorrage [hemorrhage] or some such a [–] I presume [– – – – –] such few things as he may have had and left. At least she can address our Capt. herself and she will receive all necessary information and instruction from him: Direct—

Capt. Thomas B. Green
Commanding "D" Co., 132nd
NYV Inftry
Goldsboro, N.C.

or

Else where

Letters came for him from (one) Mary Johnson and another (one) from Wallace Scott. But they were not of much consequences and I didn't think these worth sending back to their respective author, and our other reason, writing papers, envelopes and stamps are a very scarce articles among soldiers in a campaigning field — ink, pens and penholders etc. So I have destroyed them and will destroy all that may come, unless they be of some consequence, or on business importance. — Please tell the bereaved mother that Foster was respected and beloved by all in the regiment, and especially by those who knew him best and his loss is deeply mourned and more particularly in the company of which he was an Acting Orderly. His loss is deeply and sincerely felt and I can assert with much assurance that our sympathies and prayers are with her. Look up to God who giveth and taketh away. When he fell with his wound, the rebs got him, but we recaptured him. The rebs robbed him of his watch, with other little and loose affects but no money, for he had none.

I have the pleasure to be
Rev
Respectfully Your Obed't Serv't,
I. N. Parker

[ALS, Foster John Hudson Civil War Pension Record, NA]

NOTES

Editorial Procedures: Scope and Methods

1. Laurence M. Hauptman, *The Iroquois in the Civil War: From Battlefield to Reservation* (Syracuse, NY: Syracuse University Press, 1993).
2. "The Way It Was," *Niagara Frontier*, 23 (Autumn/Winter, 1976): inside front cover. Pat Virgil [Buffalo and Erie County Historical Society] to Laurence M. Hauptman, June 10, 1992 [letter in editor's possession].
3. John E. Freeman, Comp., *A Guide to Manuscripts Relating to the American Indian in the Library of the American Philosophical Society* (Philadelphia: American Philosophical Society, 1980), pp. 39, 358 [item no. 3590-3591, 3595-3597]. Martha J. Harrison [American Philosophical Society] to Laurence M. Hauptman, June 16, 1992 [letter in editor's possession]. For more information about these documents, see William N. Fenton, "Iroquois Studies at Mid-Century," *Proceedings* of the American Philosophical Society, 95 (June 12, 1951): 290-310; and George S. Snyderman, "A Preliminary Survey of American Indian Manuscripts in Repositories of the Philadelphia Area," *Proceedings* of the American Philosophical Society, 97 (October 30, 1953): 596-610.
4. Foster J. Hudson Pension Record, Civil War Pension Records, National Archives, Washington, D.C.
5. Isaac Newton Parker, Compiled Military Service Record, Records of the Adjutant General's Office, RG94, National Archives, Washington, D.C.
6. Through the efforts of George Hamell, Office of Exhibit Planning of the New York State Museum, I was able to locate this letter in a private collection. I brought this letter to the attention of James Corsaro, head of the Manuscript Division of the New York State Library, who swiftly helped acquire it for the Library.
7. Mary-Jo Kline, *A Guide to Documentary Editing* (Baltimore: Johns Hopkins University Press, 1987). I have benefited by consulting the publications of major editing projects such as Arthur S. Link et al., Eds., *The Papers of Woodrow Wilson* (Princeton: Princeton University Press, 1966-); and Lyman H. Butterfield, Ed., *Letters of Benjamin Rush* (Princeton: Princeton University Press, in cooperation with the American Philosophical Society, 1951), 2 vols.
8. Butterfield, Ed., *Letters of Benjamin Rush*, I, lxxvi.

Introduction

1. Richard Slotkin, *Gunfighter Nation: The Myth of the Frontier in Twentieth-Century America* (New York: Atheneum, 1992), pp. 12-13.
2. Bell I. Wiley, *The Life of Johnny Reb: The Common Soldier of the Confederacy* (Baton Rouge, La.: Louisiana State University Press, 1943; paperback edition, 1992), pp. 326-327; *The Life of Billy Yank: The Common Soldier of the Union* (Baton Rouge, La.: Louisiana State University Press, 1952; paperback edition, 1992), p. 318.
3. For Native Americans in the Civil War, see Annie Heloise Abel, *The American Indian as Slaveholder and Secessionist* (Cleveland: Arthur H. Clark, 1915); *The American Indian as Participant in the Civil War* (Cleveland: Arthur H. Clark, 1919); and *The American Indian Under Reconstruction* (Cleveland: Arthur H. Clark, 1925). These volumes were reprinted in a paperback edition in 1992 by the University of Nebraska Press. Alvin M. Josephy, Jr., *The Civil War in American West* (New York: Knopf, 1991). Hauptman, *The Iroquois in the Civil War*; and W. McKee Evans, *To Die Game: The Story of the Lowry Band, Indian Guerrillas of Reconstruction* (Baton Rouge, La.: Louisiana State University, 1971); William H. Armstrong, *Warrior in Two Camps: Ely S. Parker, Union General and Seneca Chief* (Syracuse, N.Y.: Syracuse University Press, 1978); Kenny A. Franks, *Stand Watie and the Agony of the Cherokee Nation* (Memphis, Tenn.: Memphis State University Press, 1979); W. David Baird, Ed., *A Creek Warrior for the Confederacy: The Autobiography of Chief G.W. Grayson* (Norman, Okla.: University of Oklahoma Press, 1988); W. Craig Gaines, *The Confederate Cherokees: John Drew's Regiment of Mounted Rifles* (Baton Rouge, La.: Louisiana State University Press, 1989); Edward J. Danziger, Jr., *Indians and Bureaucrats: Administering the Reservation Policy During the Civil War* (Urbana, Ill.: University of Illinois Press, 1974); David A. Nichols, *Lincoln and the Indians: Civil War Policy and Politics* (Columbia, Mo.: University of Missouri Press, 1978). I am currently writing a book on Native Americans in the Civil War: *Between Two Fires: American Indians in the Civil War* (New York: Free Press), forthcoming.
4. See Chart and also see Hauptman, *The Iroquois in the Civil War*, chapter 1-3.
5. Baird, Ed., *A Creek Warrior for the Confederacy*.
6. Armstrong, *Warrior in Two Camps*, pp. 7-17. I should like to thank Dr. Elisabeth Tooker for pointing out to me Parker's genealogy and correcting Armstrong's treatment of the same. M. Stagers and Co. to Newton [*sic*] Parker, Jan. 8, 1857; Ely S. Parker to Caroline Parker, July 19, 1850; Newton Parker to Ely S. Parker, Dec. 16, 1850, June 31, 1851, Oct. 15, 30, 1852; Caroline Parker to Ely S. Parker, May 29, 1850, ESP MSS, APS.

7. The photograph on page 24 was misidentified as Red Jacket, a Seneca chief (Missouri Historical Society). The one on page 23 was misidentified as Ely S. Parker (New York Public Library). I should like to thank George Hamell for bringing this new evidence to my attention. Isaac Newton Parker Enlistment Papers, June 18, 1862; "of Description of Isaac Newton Parker, 'Third Sergeant of Co. D. 132nd Reg't N.Y.S.V.' Taken From the: Descriptive Roll Book of Co. D 132 Regiment N.Y. Vol. Infantry, P. J. Claassen, Col. Commanding...", Sept. 15, 1862, both found in INP MSS, BECHS.

8. Elisabeth Tooker, "On the Development of the Handsome Lake Religion," *Proceedings* of the American Philosophical Society 133 (March 1989): 44-45; Henry S. Manley, "Buying Buffalo from the Indian," *New York History* 28 (July 1947): 313-329; Armstrong, *Warrior in Two Camps*, pp. 10-35, 64-67; 77-78. Isaac Newton Parker to Sara Jemison Parker, Aug. 17, 1862. During the American Civil War, Iroquois leaders asked Washington officials to nominate Martindale to negotiate and resolve their Kansas claims. Peter Wilson, Maris Pierce, et al. to William P. Dole, April 28, 1864, Records of the New York Agency, OIA, M234, MR590, RG75, NA.

9. Lewis Henry Morgan, *The League of the Ho-de-no-sau-nee, or Iroquois* (Rochester, NY, 1851; paperback reprint, New York: Corinth Books, 1962). Lewis Henry Morgan to Newton Parker, Dec. 19, 1849, Nov. 4, 1851; Caroline Parker to Ely S. Parker, July 5, 1853, ESP MSS, APS. Lewis Henry Morgan to General Benjamin Butler, Dec. 14, 1863, found in Compiled Military Service Record of Isaac Newton Parker, Records of the Adjutant General's Office, RG94, NA. See also footnote 60 and Thomas R. Trautmann, *Lewis Henry Morgan and the Invention of Kinship* (Berkeley, Calif.: University of California Press, 1987), pp. 36-57; Elisabeth Tooker, *Lewis Henry Morgan on Iroquois Material Culture* (Tucson: University of Arizona Press, 1994).

10. Arthur C. Parker, *The Life of General Ely S. Parker, Last Grand Sachem of the Iroquois and General Grant's Military Secretary*. Publications of the Buffalo Historical Society 23 (Buffalo, 1919), pp. 100, 189. For Newt Parker's escapades, also see Armstrong, *Warrior in Two Camps*, pp. 56-57, 139; Newton [*sic*] Parker to Caroline Parker, Aug. 7, 1853; Caroline Parker to Ely S. Parker, Feb. 15, 1855, April 5, 1859; Chauncey C. Jemison to Caroline Parker, Nov. 30, 1854; Theron Seymour to Ely S. Parker, Dec. 11, 1854, ESP MSS, APS.

11. Isaac Newton Parker to Sara Jemison, March 1, Nov. 1, 1860, Jan. 25, Sept. 3, 1861, INP MSS, BECHS; Caroline [Carrie] Parker to Sarah Jemison, April 7, 1855, March 20, 1858, INP MSS, BECHS.

12. Isaac Newton Parker to Sarah Jemison, Nov. 28, 1859, Jan. 25, Oct. 17, 1860, Jan. 3, Feb. 6, 18, 26, March 1, 1861. INP MSS, BECHS. Please note that Newt Parker spelled his wife's first name with and without the letter "h."

13. Isaac Newton Parker to Sara Jemison, Jan. 31, 1860, INP MSS, BECHS.

14. Isaac Newton Parker to Sara Jemison, Feb. 26, 1861, INP MSS, BECHS.

15. Isaac Newton Parker to Sara Jemison, Jan. 25, 1861; Sara Jemison to Isaac Newton Parker, Jan. 31, 1860, INP MSS, BECHS.

16. Isaac Newton Parker to Sarah Jemison, Oct. 17, 1860, INP MSS, BECHS.
17. Isaac Newton Parker to Sara Jemison, Feb. 18, 1860, INP MSS, BECHS. See also Isaac Newton Parker to Sara Jemison, Jan. 25, 1860, INP MSS, BECHS.
18. Isaac Newton Parker to Sara Jemison, Feb. 26, 1861, INP MSS, BECHS.
19. Isaac Newton Parker to Sara Jemison Parker, April 29, 1861, INP MSS, BECHS.
20. Isaac Newton Parker to Sara Jemison Parker, June 13, 1861, INP MSS, BECHS.
21. Isaac Newton Parker to Sara Jemison Parker, Sept. 3, 1861, INP MSS, BECHS. See Armstrong, *Warrior in Two Camps*, pp. 58-68.
22. Isaac Newton Parker to Sara Jemison Parker, Jan. 31, 1861, INP MSS, BECHS.
23. Isaac Newton Parker to Sara Jemison Parker, April 20, 1862, INP MSS, BECHS.
24. Isaac Newton Parker to Sara Jemison, Jan. 25, 1860, INP MSS, BECHS. For Levi, see Armstrong, *Warrior in Two Camps*, pp. 10, 54, 80, 105, 188-192.
25. Isaac Newton Parker to Sara Jemison Parker, Sept. 3, 1861, INP MSS, BECHS. Parker was rejected for a commission in the Regular Army after the Civil War because of failing eyesight.
26. Isaac Newton Parker to Sara Jemison Parker, March 4, 1862, INP MSS, BECHS.
27. Isaac Newton Parker to Sara Jemison, Oct. 17, 1860, INP MSS, BECHS.
28. Isaac Newton Parker to Sara Jemison Parker, Feb. 26, March 1, Dec. 28, 1861, INP MSS, BECHS. The editor should like to thank Ms. Abigail Laura Wheeler, Nicholson Parker's great-granddaughter and a Cayuga Indian member of the [Asher] Wright Memorial Church at the Cattaraugus Indian Reservation for aiding me in this search.
29. Descriptive Muster Rolls, Regimental Books, D Company, 132nd NYS Volunteer Infantry, Records of the Adjutant General's Office, RG94, NA. See Chart.
30. Hauptman, *The Iroquois and the Civil War*, chapter 1; Armstrong, *Warrior in Two Camps*, pp. 80-83. Isaac Newton Parker to Sara Jemison Parker, Oct. 9, 1861, INP MSS, BECHS. It should be noted that both the "federal government and the State of New York initially displayed either indifference or hostility or both to the suggestion of using black volunteers to fight the South." William Seraile, "The Struggle to Raise Black Regiments in New York State," *New-York Historical Society Quarterly* 58 (July 1974): 215.
31. Hugh Hastings, Comp., "One Hundred and Thirty Second Regiment of Infantry," Grand Army of the Republic Collection, New York State Library, Manuscript Division, Albany. Hastings was the New York State Historian and compiled this regimental history based on the notes made by Claassen and Cusick. Hastings later published some of this material in: *Second Annual Report* [of the New York State Historian] (Albany, 1897), Appendix F.
32. See Chart. For official citations of Iroquois heroism, see *OR*, ser. 1, vol. 33, pp. 60-76; ser. 1, vol. 40, pt. 1, p. 814. See also New York State Historian, *Second Annual Report*, Appendix F; and Peter J. Claassen to Whom It May Concern, Jan. 14, 1865, Cornelius C. Cusick's ACP Branch Document File 1888, Box 1168, Records of the Adjutant General's Office, RG94, NA. For a contrast with African American troops, see Virginia M. Adams, Ed., *On the Altar of Freedom: A Black Soldier's Civil War Letters from the Front: Corpo-*

ral James Henry Gooding (Amherst, Mass.: University of Massachusetts Press, 1991). Please note that at least one Tuscarora soldier served in a segregated unit—Clinton Mountpleasant—who was transferred from the 30th New York to the 31st United States Colored Regiment.

33. Hauptman, *The Iroquois in the Civil War*, chapter 3. For Cusick's own account of the 132nd New York State Volunteers, see two of his unpublished accounts of the fighting in North Carolina: "Operations of the Confederate Forces Under Major General George E. Pickett, Against New Berne, N.C. February 1-4, 1864. The 132nd N.Y. Interposes" and his "North Carolina[:] the fight near Kinston, N.C. The Rebels badly used up— Our troops march seventy-three miles in thirty-nine hours," Aug. 2, 1896, GAR Collection MSS, 132nd New York State Volunteer Infantry, Package 14, NYSL. For the lobbying effort to secure Iroquois admission to military service, see C. [Chauncey] C. Jemison to Isaac Newton Parker, Aug. 5, 1862, NYSL. Isaac Newton Parker to Sara Jemison Parker, Nov. 12, 1861, INP MSS, BECHS. Ely S. Parker to William P. Dole [Commissioner of Indian Affairs], March 5, 1862, Dole to Parker, March 12, 1862, Records of the New York Agency, OIA, M234, MR590, RG75, NA. Colonel John Fisk to Ely S. Parker, April 4, 1862, ESP MSS, APS. Cornelius C. Cusick to Abraham Lincoln, Jan. 23, 1865, [Cusick's] ACP Branch Document File 1888, Box 1168, Records of the Office of the Adjutant General, RG94, NA.

34. Hauptman, *The Iroquois in the Civil War*, chapter 3. Cornelius C. Cusick to Adjutant General U.S. Army, April 2, 1883, [Cusick's] ACP Branch Document File, 1888, Box 1168, Records of the Adjutant General's Office, RG94, NA. New York State Historian, 2nd Annual Report, Appendix F. Cornelius C. Cusick, Pension Record, Lizzie B. Cusick's [wife's] pension application 800,281, certificate 587,550, Civil War Pension Records, NA. Cusick died on January 3, 1904. Elias Johnson, *Legends, Traditions and Laws, of the Iroquois* or *Six Nations, and History of the Tuscarora Indians* (Lockport, NY: Union Printing & Publishing Co., 1881), pp. 171-172; E. Roy Johnson, *The Tuscaroras: History-Traditions-Culture* (Murfreesboro, NC: Johnson Publishing Co., 1968), II, 228-229; Barbara Graymont, Ed., *Fighting Tuscarora: The Autobiography of Chief Clinton Rickard* (Syracuse, N.Y.: Syracuse University Press, 1973). I should like to thank Professor Barbara Graymont for sharing with me her special knowledge about the Cusick-Rickard family and Tuscarora history. For the accusations against Cusick and Jemison, see the letter reprinted in this edition: C. C. Jemison to Isaac Newton Parker, Aug. 5, 1862, NYSL.

35. Isaac Newton Parker to Sara Jemison Parker, Aug. 17, 1862, INP MSS, BECHS.

36. Gerald E. Wheeler and A. Stuart Pitt, "The 53rd New York: A Zoo-Zoo Tale," *New York History* 37 (Oct. 1956): 415-420. Descriptive Muster Roll, D Company, 132nd NYS Volunteer Infantry; Morning Reports, 1863-1865 (Monthly Summaries), D Company, 132nd NYS Volunteer Infantry, Records of the Adjutant General's Office, RG75, NA. Isaac Newton Parker to Sara Jemison Parker, Aug. 17, 1862, Dec. 24, 1862, INP MSS, BECHS.

37. Hastings, Comp., "One Hundred and Thirty Second Regiment of Infantry."
38. Ibid.; Isaac Newton Parker, Compiled Military Service Record, Records of the Adjutant General's Office, RG94, NA; Isaac Newton Parker to Sara Jemison Parker, Feb. 3, Dec. 27, 1863, INP MSS, BECHS; Isaac Newton Parker to Caroline Parker, June 26, 1864, ESP MSS, APS; Armstrong, *Warrior in Two Camps*, pp. 82, 104-105.
39. Isaac Newton Parker to Sara Jemison Parker, Aug. 17, 1862, Jan. 15, Feb. 3, 26, April 3, May 17, Oct. 5, 18, 1863; Isaac Newton Parker to Martha Hoyt Parker, Aug. 15, 1863, INP MSS, BECHS. For a comparison, see Joseph T. Glatthaar, *Forged in Battle: The Civil War Alliance of Black Soldiers and White Officers* (New York: The Free Press, 1990). After the war, the Indians in the company were falsely accused of scalping Confederates in 1864. Their white comrades-in-arms came to their defense: Dudley A. Beekman to Hugh Hastings, March 21, 1897; A. Luersen to Hastings, May 23, 1897, GAR MSS, 132nd New York State Volunteer Infantry, Package 14, NYSL.
40. Isaac Newton Parker to Martha Hoyt Parker, April 1, 1864, ESP MSS, APS.
41. Hastings, Comp., "One Hundred and Thirty Second Regiment of Infantry." Armstrong, *Warrior in Two Camps*, p. 104. Armstrong maintains that 35 soldiers were killed in the explosion of the torpedo mines.
42. Isaac Newton Parker to Sara Jemison Parker, Dec. 1, 1862, Jan. 15, 1863, undated letter, early 1863, Feb. 3, 20, 26, April 3, May 17, Oct. 5, 18, Nov. 4, Dec. 27, 1863; Jan. 3, 1864, INP MSS, BECHS. For the details of the bounty controversy of 1863 and 1864 which involved underage and other Iroquois recruits, see Hauptman, *The Iroquois and the Civil War*, chapter 8.
43. Isaac Newton Parker to Sara Jemison Parker, June 21, 1863, INP MSS, BECHS.
44. Isaac Newton Parker to Martha Hoyt Parker, April 1, 1864, ESP MSS, APS.
45. Isaac Newton Parker to Sara Jemison Parker, June 6, 1864, ESP MSS, APS.
46. Isaac Newton Parker to Sara Jemison Parker, Oct. 18, 1863, INP MSS, BECHS.
47. Isaac Newton Parker to Sara Jemison Parker, Dec. 20, 1863, INP MSS, BECHS.
48. Lewis Henry Morgan to General Benjamin Butler, Dec. 14, 1863.
49. John G. Barrett, *The Civil War in North Carolina* (Chapel Hill, N.C.: University of North Carolina Press, 1961), pp. 203-212.
50. Ibid.
51. Ibid. The battle can be traced in *OR*, ser. I, v. 33, Part I: pp. 60-76.
52. *OR*, ser. I, v. 33, Part I: p. 62.
53. Ibid. p. 76.
54. R. Emmett Fiske to Whom It May Concern, Jan. 13, 1865, [Cusick's] ACP Branch Document, File 1888, Box 1168, Records of the Adjutant General's Office, RG94, NA.
55. Isaac Newton Parker Map of Union Forces at New Bern and Notes of Battle of Batchelder's Creek, Feb. 1, 1864 and other notes, May 10, 1864, ESP MSS, APS. Descriptive Muster Roll, Regimental Books, D Company, 132nd NYS Volunteer Infantry, Records of the Adjutant General's Office, RG75, NA; Pension Record of William Kennedy, certificate #308,776, application #519,187, "Widow Kennedy, mother of William Kennedy," CWPR, NA.

56. *OR*, Ser. I, 40, Part 1: 814-816.
57. New York State Historian, *2nd Annual Report*, Appendix F; Peter J. Claassen to Whom It May Concern, Jan. 14, 1865, [Cusick's] ACP Branch Document File 1888, Box 1168, Records of the Adjutant General's Office, RG94, NA.
58. Isaac Newton Parker to Asher Wright, April 1, 1865, Foster John Hudson Pension Records, mother's application (Louisa Johnnyjohn Hudson), CWPR, NA. Asher Wright served the Seneca from 1831 to 1875 and was a major force in education, religious life, and social welfare of the Indians in western New York. For Wright's missionary work among the Seneca, see Thomas S. Abler, "Protestant Missionaries and Native Cultures: Parallel Careers of Asher Wright and Silas T. Rand," *American Indian Quarterly* 16 (Winter 1992): 25-38; and William N. Fenton, "Toward the Gradual Civilization of the Indian Natives: The Missionary and Linguistic Work of Asher Wright (1803-1875) Among the Senecas of Western New York," *Proceedings* of the American Philosophical Society 100 (Dec. 1956): 567-581.
59. See Chart.
60. Quoted in John Y. Simon, Ed., *The Papers of Ulysses S. Grant* (Carbondale, Ill.: Southern Illinois Press, 1991), XVII: 408.
61. Ibid., pp. 407-408.
62. Armstrong, *Warrior in Two Camps*, p. 139; H. Craig Miner, *The Corporation and the Indian* (Columbia, MO: University of Missouri Press, 1976), pp. 27-28; Grant Foreman, *The Last Trek of the Indians* (Chicago: University of Chicago Press, 1946; reprint edition, New York: Russell and Russell, 1972), p. 339 n 50; Parker, *The Life of General Ely S. Parker*, p. 189. There is an undated newsclipping in the Lewis Henry Morgan MSS at the University of Rochester Library which mentions the offer of a military commission to Parker at the end of the Civil War. I should like to thank Dr. Elisabeth Tooker for bringing this newsclipping to my attention.
63. Parker, *The Life of Ely S. Parker*, p. 191.

Letters

1. Hattie Two Guns is frequently referred to in Newt Parker's letters. Besides teaching at Cattaraugus and Tonawanda, she later was employed as a teacher of freedmen by the American Missionary Society. I thank Rev. William H. Armstrong for his help in identifying "Hatt."

2. Edwin Denison Morgan was Governor of New York from 1858 to 1862. A New York City grocer, merchant, and banker, he was a Whig who later joined the Republican Party. He was commissioned Major General in September of 1861.

3. This letter is one of only two in the collection to refer to Isaac's and Sara's son Trent. There is no information known about him.

4. "Colonel Shepard" is probably Lieutenant Colonel Oliver Lathrop Shepherd who was a West Point graduate and veteran of the Mexican War. He was on mustering duty in New York from June to December, 1861. Carlos Adolphus Waite, the "old man," served in the regular army from 1820 to 1864. He fought in the Mexican War and was a colonel in the 1st United States Infantry during the Civil War. Private Samuel G. Isaacs, known as "Big Ike," was the foremost Indian sharpshooter of D Company, 132nd New York State Volunteer Infantry during the Civil War. "Capt. C. C. Jemison" is probably Chauncey C. Jemison, a teacher and farmer as well as an old family friend of the Parker family, whose letters are included in the Ely S. Parker MSS in the APS. Hauptman, *The Iroquois and the Civil War*, chapter 2; Mark M. Boatner III, *The Civil War Dictionary*, Revised (New York: McKay, 1988; paperback edition, New York: Vintage Books, 1991), pp. 746, 883.

5. The Empire Brigade was raised by Francis B. Spinola, a Democratic Party loyalist in New York. He served as general from October, 1862 to June 8, 1865. Boatner, *The Civil War Dictionary*, pp. 782-783. For Spinola, see also Eugene Converse Murdock, *Patriotism Limited, 1862-1865: The Civil War Draft and the Bounty System* (Kent, Ohio: Kent State University Press, 1967), pp. 172-186.

6. Robert Sanford Foster, 1834-1903, was a Union general who later "served on the military commission that tried Lincoln's assassins." Boatner, *The Civil War Dictionary*, p. 302. He should not be confused with General John G. Foster, 1823-1874, who served as Parker's commanding general in North Carolina (pp. 74-75, 81-83).

7. James Jourdan, born in Ireland, rose in rank from major to general during the Civil War. Boatner, *The Civil War Dictionary*, p. 446.

8. Underage recruits, mostly the sons of poor Indian farmers, were enticed off the Seneca reservations in New York to join the Union army and navy by promises of financial remuneration. This led to an Iroquois chiefs meeting with

President Abraham Lincoln in November, 1863 to secure their release from service. Most of the recruits remained in service until the end of the war since they could not pay back the bounty enticements that were given to them upon enlistment. See Laurence M. Hauptman, "Samuel George (1795-1873): A Study of Onondaga Indian Conservatism," *New York History* 71 (January 1989): 15-19.

9. At the top of the page of the original letter, Isaac Newton Parker crudely drew an illustration of a pocket watch.

10. This remarkable letter differs in handwriting from the other letters in this collection. It was apparently written down by another soldier in the Tuscarora Company or was transcribed by Parker's family at some other time. The author believes it to be authentic based upon the events described as well as his knowledge of the regimental history of 132nd New York State Volunteers and Iroquois history. John James Peck, 1821-1878, was a railroad and banking magnate active in Democratic Party politics. He served in the Mexican War, on the frontier, and as a general for the Union from August, 1861 to August, 1865. Boatner, *The Civil War Dictionary*, p. 629. A Parrott gun was a "rifled, muzzle-loading cannon, varying in size from 3-inch (10-pound shell) to 10-inch (250-pound projectile invented by R. P. Parrott." Parrott was the Superintendent of West Point Iron and Cannon Foundry from 1836 to 1867. Boatner, *The Civil War Dictionary*, p. 621. Martha Hoyt was married to Isaac Newton Parker's older brother Nicholson. Nicholson Parker temporarily deserted his wife around 1877. He later returned to his family. Martha and Nicholson had five children. Martha was a white woman who was the niece of Laura Wright, missionary to the Seneca. [Armstrong, *Warrior in Two Camps*, pp. 186-187.]

11. Dr. Peter Wilson, a Cayuga Indian, was a graduate of Geneva Medical College. A licensed physician, he also served on several occasions as interpreter for the Seneca Indians in the 1840s and 1850s. He was active in encouraging Indian recruitment during the Civil War. See Hauptman, *The Iroquois and the Civil War*, chapter 1. Edward Green was a Tonawanda Seneca farmer who enlisted on June 28, 1862. He received a disability discharge on September 15, 1863 and died of consumption in 1866. Edward Green Pension Record, Civil War Pension Records, NA. Quincy Adams Gillmore, 1825-1888, was a Union general and teacher of military engineering at West Point. He commanded the X Corps and the Department of the South at Charleston, South Carolina from June, 1863 to May, 1864. Boatner, *The Civil War Dictionary*, p. 343.

INDEX

116